CACTI

CACTI

An Illustrated Guide to over 150 Representative Species

Marcus Schneck

SHOOTING STAR PRESS

A QUINTET BOOK

This edition published in 1995 for:
Shooting Star Press, Inc.
230 Fifth Avenue, Suite 1212
New York, NY 10001

ISBN 1-57335-303-5

This book was designed and produced by
Quintet Publishing Limited
6 Blundell Street
London N7 9BH

Creative Director: Richard Dewing
Designer: Nicola Chapman
Project Editor: Damian Thompson
Copy Editor: Anne Cree
Picture Researchers:
Marcus Schneck and Damian Thompson
Illustrator: Danny McBride

Typeset in Great Britain by
Central Southern Typesetters, Eastbourne
Manufactured in Singapore by
Eray Scan Pte. Ltd
Printed in Singapore by
Star Standard Industries (Pte) Ltd

Contents

Introduction

The cactus is perhaps one of the most evocative members of the plant kingdom. It inspires visions of tall prickly columns of green reaching skyward from the deserts of the American West, while cowboys and Indians battle it out with each other under the blazing sun.

Of course, we have all been indoctrinated with this Hollywood version of the American West, complete with cacti as a central player. Fortunately for we devotees of John Wayne, this is not entirely a false image; it is just an incomplete one.

HABITAT

The American West, both in its cowboy-past and oil-field-present, is one of the main habitats in which cacti grow — often in profusion. But it is far from being the only cacti-rich environment in the world.

Species of these plants, a type of succulent, are found from watery, tropical jungles to the driest deserts, and from just above sea-level with salt-spray misting around their spines, to the tallest mountaintops where they are occasionally hidden beneath a coating of snow.

Through thousands of years of evolution, species of cacti have emerged to inhabit as wide a range of environments as possible. However, only a relatively small number of species actually make their homes in regions that can be classified as true desert (i.e. receiving less than 10 inches of rainfall per year).

Nevertheless, a surprising variety of species have come to live on rocky, mountain slopes, often taking advantage of tiny nooks and crannies among the rocks that other plants could not find a foothold in. Generally, the soil where such cacti occur tends to be quite well-drained, protecting the plants from an excess of moisture.

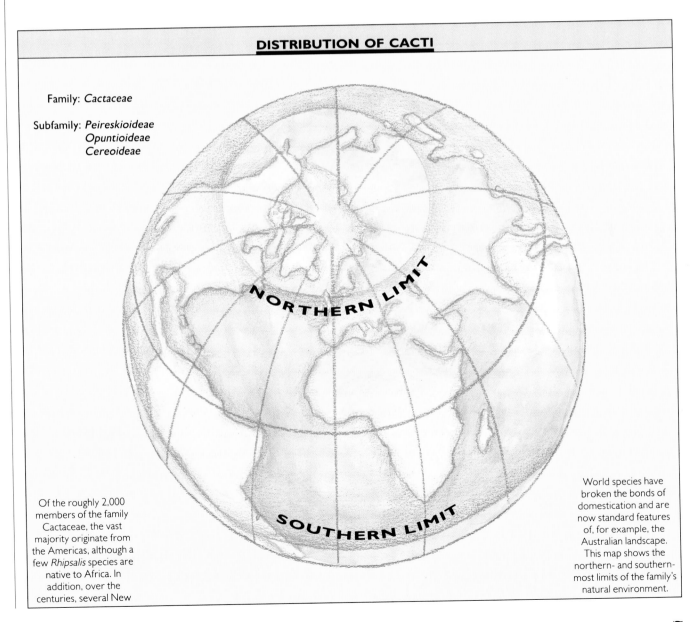

DISTRIBUTION OF CACTI

Family: *Cactaceae*

Subfamily: *Peireskioideae*
Opuntioideae
Cereoideae

NORTHERN LIMIT

SOUTHERN LIMIT

Of the roughly 2,000 members of the family Cactaceae, the vast majority originate from the Americas, although a few *Rhipsalis* species are native to Africa. In addition, over the centuries, several New

World species have broken the bonds of domestication and are now standard features of, for example, the Australian landscape. This map shows the northern- and southern-most limits of the family's natural environment.

TOPOGRAPHICAL AND CLIMATIC DATA

Examples of topographical and climatic data from natural habitats of cacti in North and South America (after *World Atlas of Climate* 1967)

Region	Altitude above sea-level (FEET)	Annual mean temperature (°FAHRENHEIT)	Annual rainfall (INCHES)	Frost incidence
Tucson (ARIZONA)	1378	67	11¾ (w)*	Yes
Chihuahua (MEXICO)	4669	65	15¾ (s)*	Yes
Durango (MEXICO)	6198	63	19¼ (s)	Yes
Zacatecas (MEXICO)	8570	56	14½ (s)	Yes
San Louis Potosi (MEXICO)	4518	64	14¼ (s)	Yes
Leon (MEXICO)	5935	65	26½ (s)	Yes
Queretaro (MEXICO)	6079	64	20 (s)	Yes
Mexico City (MEXICO)	7480	60	23½ (s)	No
La Paz (S CALIFORNIA)	59	76	7 (w)	No
Lima (PERU)	518	67	2 (w)	No
Taltal (CHILE)	128	63	½ (w)	No
Coquimbo (CHILE)	89	58	4½ (w)	No
Arequipa (PERU)	8041	57	4⅕ (s)	No
Cajamarca (PERU)	9219	58	45¾ (s)	No
Cochabamba (BOLIVIA)	8448	63	18½ (s)	No
Potosi (BOLIVIA)	9350	54	26½ (s)	No
Jujuy (ARGENTINA)	4167	63	29¾ (s)	No
Salta (ARGENTINA)	4003	64	28½ (s)	No
Tucuman (ARGENTINA)	1578	66	39 (s)	No
Catamarca (ARGENTINA)	1795	69	14⅕ (s)	No
Montes Claros (BRAZIL)	2018	71	50 (s)	No
Parana (ARGENTINA)	213	65	35 (s)	No
Rio de Janeiro (BRAZIL)	197	74	44 (s)	No
Santos (BRAZIL)	10	71	83 (s+w)	No

Notes: *S = mainly summer
*W = mainly winter

▲

Unlike forest regions, the desert offers very little to deflect the sun's rays from the surface during the day and equally little to prevent heat dispersion from the heated soil at night. An understanding of this can be helpful in raising more healthy plants.

A forest of giant saguaro cacti is the typical vision that many of us have of the place of origin for our cacti, perpetuated through such media as the American western movie.

▼

a

Other species have developed mechanisms for capturing the limited amounts of moisture they need from the air of coastal regions. The spines collect the moisture, which eventually beads and drops to the soil where the roots suck it in. As with any plant forced to subsist on surface moisture, the root systems of these cacti are generally shallow but very widespread.

There are more than 2,000 members of the family Cactaceae. With a very few exceptions, they all originate from the New World, although a few *Rhipsalis* species are native to Africa, and several American species have broken the bonds of domestication over the past several centuries to gain a firm foothold on other continents. Some of these species have become so firmly entrenched in their new homelands that most casual observers view them as part of the natural landscape. Parts of Australia are a prime example of this, where several species of *Opuntia* have even become nuisance weeds. Many cacti seem to fall into that broad category of organisms that have been transplanted – either accidentally or intentionally – into new environments, where they flourished.

The four basic structures that cacti commonly take are: a) globular (*Obregonia denegrei*); b) columnar (*Stenocereus weberi*); c) leaf-like or pad (*Opuntia basilaris*); and d) elongated/prostrate (*Heliocereus speciosus*).

c

b

d

Areoles, like the felt-covered triangles across the surface of the stem of this *Borzicactus madisoniorum*, are one of the keys to identification of a species. In the majority of species the spines grow from the areoles.

The various parts of a cactus flower are easy to differentiate on this *Echinocereus sciurus*. The petals are the pinkish structures, the stamen anthers are creamy yellow, the stamen filaments are greenish-yellow, and the stigma, which caps the pistil, is dark green.

RANGE

Humans have been fascinated by these strange plants for many centuries. A wide variety of cacti were included in the prized collections of rulers of the ancient but advanced native American civilizations. And, even before that time, more primitive native cultures were discovering myriad uses – food, medicine, ornamentation and everyday appliance – for the cacti that filled their environment.

Europeans first encountered cacti in the form of the *Melocactus* species, in the 16th century. In 1753 Linnaeus placed this (which he labelled *Cactus melocactus*), and 20 other species into the genus *Cactus* in his taxonomic system of relating like organisms to one another.

The incredible range of natural habitats from which cacti originate means that anyone who is so inclined can find at least a few species of cacti that are perfectly suited to the spot where he or she wants to grow them. Given this, we can see that even the northerly temperate climates with their heavy frosts and snowfalls can present growing opportunities – even for outdoor cacti gardens. And it requires little thought for us to realise that nearly any indoor location can also have its resident cactus species. This, together with mechanisms like greenhouses or even simpler devices, means that virtually any species of cacti can be grown in and around the home. Sophisticated lighting fixtures can even eliminate the need for natural light.

Illustrations of an *Opuntia*-like plant, similar to these *Opuntia erinacea*, first appeared in the 1635 *Historia de las Indias Occidentales* by Gonzalo Hernandez de Oviedo y Valdez.

A wide variety of cacti grow very nicely in pots. For many species, which cannot survive the colder months in more northerly climes, this makes for easy transport from outdoors to in.

▲

Man has found many non-ornamental uses for cacti. One of the strangest is cactus jelly, which actually rivals in taste more domestic and widely known spreads.

The brilliant and profuse flowers of many cacti species are an added bonus to many neophytes.

In addition, throughout the more tropical regions of the world, cacti are an excellent choice for carefree landscape gardening, where other types of greenery would soon fade and die without a continuous infusion of water. Once established on site, many species of cacti can be left on their own to draw what they need from the existing environment. As a matter of fact, some gardeners in these regions have reduced their use of water in the garden by 50 per cent or more with the installation of cacti.

CHARACTERISTICS

As I did when I first started pursuing an interest in cacti, you too may equate spines with cacti and cacti with spines. In other words, if it has spines it must be a cactus.

However, that statement is not strictly true. Although most species of cacti do have spines, there are also many other succulents, and other types of plants, that have spines and yet are not cacti, just as there are a considerable number of cacti, such as many of the *Lophophora* species, that are spineless.

Size, too, is not a good determinant of whether a plant is or is not a cactus. From the miniatures of the cacti world, which reach the size of a thimble at full maturity, to towering, tree-like giants that can grow to more than 80 feet in height, the range in cacti species is as great as anything to be found elsewhere in the plant kingdom.

▲
The one characteristic that most people instantly recognize in cacti is their spines. Avoiding direct contact with the plant is always the best way to keep from literally getting "stuck" on it.

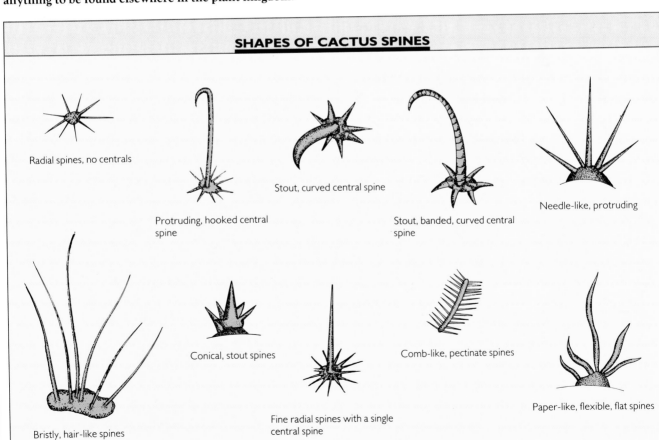

SHAPES OF CACTUS SPINES

Radial spines, no centrals

Protruding, hooked central spine

Stout, curved central spine

Stout, banded, curved central spine

Needle-like, protruding

Bristly, hair-like spines

Conical, stout spines

Fine radial spines with a single central spine

Comb-like, pectinate spines

Paper-like, flexible, flat spines

However, with few exceptions, most cacti do share a number of characteristics. For instance, most do not have leaves in the usual sense of the word. The surface of the plant is generally ribbed or tuberculate, with felt-covered areoles appearing on these structures. The spines of the plant grow from these areoles, as do new growths and often the flowers.

OBTAINING SEEDS

Nearly all cacti flowers have both male and female parts. This condition is called hermaphroditic. For fertilization to take place, pollen must be transferred from the stamens (the male parts of the flower) to the stigma at the tip of the pistil.

Just as with many other plant families the scent and taste of the flowers and their nectar attract insects. As the insects draw their food from the flowers, pollen adheres to their bodies. Unintentionally they carry that pollen to the next flower they visit, depositing some of it onto the stigma there. Some large-flowering species of cacti even employ birds and bats in this process.

From fertilization, the seeds begin developing in the ovary, which eventually produces the seed-filled fruit. In some species, the fruit dries, cracks and releases the seeds. In many others, the fruit is very fleshy and moist, attracting birds and small creatures to feast upon it. The seeds are later released in the excrement of these creatures. Although in the wild only a small number of seeds will actually fall among favourable and fertile conditions, even that small amount is generally enough to perpetuate the species.

Under cultivation conditions – and particularly indoors – human hands must replace the insects, birds and bats.

▲

In shopping for new cacti, look for specimens that appear to have healthy colour and normal form, as well as a vigorous pattern of growth.

SHAPES OF CACTUS FLOWERS

(cross section)

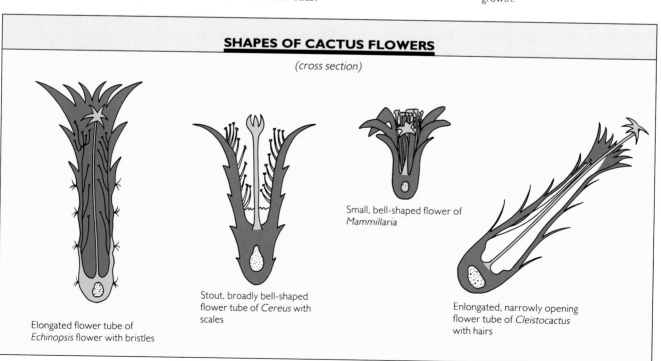

Elongated flower tube of *Echinopsis* flower with bristles

Stout, broadly bell-shaped flower tube of *Cereus* with scales

Small, bell-shaped flower of *Mammillaria*

Enlongated, narrowly opening flower tube of *Cleistocactus* with hairs

ANATOMY OF A CACTUS FLOWER

Stigma, divided into lobes

Pollen-bearing stamens

Flower petals

Seed-bearing ovary

A small, thin paintbrush is the generally accepted tool. The gardener can then simply touch the bristled portion of the brush to the stigma of the open flower and then the pistil of another flower. However, avoid moisture at all costs during the process, as damp pollen is generally ruined pollen.

In some cacti species the transfer can be done within the same flower. In many others, however, it must be between different flowers or different plants.

The way in which you gather the seeds for your own use in growing new specimens will depend on the species with which you're working. For those species that tend to disburse their seeds when the fruit dries and cracks open, you may want to tie a very finely meshed sack about the fruit to catch the seeds. For the more fleshy fruited species you should harvest the fruit when ripe and open it to remove and dry the seeds.

Under proper conditions, dried cacti seeds will be usable for several years after their harvest. In their natural environment this ability is crucial in allowing the seeds to lie in wait for just the right conditions to release their

► Generating a new plant from many branching-type species can be as easy as cutting off one of the new branches at its base and planting the base in a pot of dry soil. The *Opuntia* and *Cereus* species are particularly well-suited for this cultivation technique.

new growth – conditions that might be years in the offing. Proper conditions – cool, dry and protected from insects – are easily achieved by sealing the seeds in airtight plastic freezer bags and storing them at the back of a top shelf in the refrigerator. Zipper-type bags seem to allow for easiest and most thorough manual removal of the air.

A huge variety of seeds are available commercially through mail-order and retail outlets. With increasing competition in the field of commercial horticulture it is reasonably safe to assume that any company that has survived for a few years can be relied upon to supply seeds of good quality.

One commonly available item that should be religiously avoided is the mixed package of cacti seeds. Usually these display a wonderland of cacti variety on their packages. And therein lies the problem. Yes, all those different sizes and shapes of cacti do look fantastic together. But they probably were not grown that way. What the illustration does not reflect is the very different growing conditions needed for all the different species. In many ways it is a deadly mix. If you follow the packet's instructions you will supply enough water for the fast-growing species to spring to life – and more than enough water to drown and rot the slower-growing species.

A much more fruitful approach is to buy single-species packets, or at least mixed packets of very similar species, and to grow each under the conditions best suited to their propagation needs. Attractive displays can be put together by placing the different pots in a variety of pleasing arrangements.

▲ ▶
Would-be cactus growers and hobbyists in the western USA have a wealth of detailed instruction available to them in the form of the many public cacti gardens that can be found throughout the region. In the UK, specialised greenhouses must serve this purpose.

▶
Elaborate landscapes, sometimes called desertscapes, can be created entirely of cacti species. Such a garden will require up to 50 per cent less water.

GERMINATION

Only two factors are crucial in getting the freshly planted seeds to germinate: water and temperature. Having placed the seeds in the soil give them a good drenching, but after that they must be kept moist not wet. A further soaking is likely to cause rot, whereas even a brief drying out will cut off the plant's growth forever. Generally, temperatures should not be allowed to fall below 70°F (21°C), nor rise to more than 90°F (32°C). As countless gardeners have discovered with many types of plants, the top of a refrigerator generally maintains these optimum conditions.

The operation becomes a little more complicated when the young plant emerges from the soil. Correct water and temperature conditions must be maintained, as with the seeds, but now the tender young plant must be protected from the direct rays of the sun. Although the seedling needs sunlight, it must be shaded at all times from its direct rays. In addition, the young plant needs a constant circulation of warm air about it.

Both of these measures provide excellent growing conditions for the cacti, while at the same time thwarting the growth of mosses, fungi and bacteria. All of these organisms, if given proper conditions, will grow much faster than even the fastest-growing cacti and take over the growing medium. While initial growing periods of 6–18 months are not uncommon for cacti species, mossy, fungal or bacterial growth can be well along within days.

GROWING MEDIUMS AND TOOLS

For this same reason, everything involved in the growing of young cacti must be sterilized – the growing medium, pots, tools – everything that could introduce the spores of the above offenders.

The gardener must start with a growing medium made up of one part dry leaf mould (with all unrotted organic matter removed) that is ground into a fine dust, one part gritty sand, and one part ultra-fine grit. To obtain the correct sizings of these elements, an ordinary sieve from the kitchen can be used. Run the elements through the sieve and keep the leaf mould that doesn't fall through, plus the sand and grit that does fall through.

These elements should be mixed and blended thoroughly, and then sterilized by baking in a covered pan in the oven. To the sterilized mixture, a touch of commercially available granular fertilizer can be blended in.

Commercially available potting mixtures generally need to have some gritty material added to them to be suitable for cacti, otherwise they simply won't be well-drained enough. Also, the gardener might consider home-sterilizing them – even when their labels state that they are already sterilized.

After the pot is filled with the growing medium and the cactus seeds have been planted, place a very thin layer of coarser grit across the top of the soil to keep everything in place. This also helps to prevent the growth of the undesirables.

The water used with your young cacti should also be sterile. This can be achieved by buying distilled water or by boiling tapwater (be certain to bring it to a full, rolling boil). For the initial soaking of the seeds, immediately after planting, a mild, water-soluble, non-systemic fungicide should be added to the water. This same treatment can be repeated every now and then in the regular waterings of the seeds and later of the young plants.

Tools and plastic pots (plastic being the preferred material for starting cacti) should be washed with soapy water, rinsed thoroughly and then dropped into boiling water. The gardener should obtain tools and pots that can withstand this kind of treatment.

Some of the faster-growing cacti species will be ready for transfer into a more nutrient-rich (containing more rotted leaf mould), medium within a few months. However, many species will be much too fragile for transfer for many months. Some need to be maintained in the initial growing medium and pot for as much as a year and a half. A good rule of thumb is this: If it appears too fragile to be handled, it probably is. Throughout this period, it is important to maintain a constant shading for the tender young plants.

In warmer, drier climates, sealed systems may prove beneficial in getting plants started. Following all the sterilization, shading and warmth precautions oulined earlier, an initial watering followed by a sealing of the container might be all the seeds need to achieve germination. Of course, the containers must be opened as soon as seedlings emerge to prevent rotting, and growth of undesirables.

Regardless of how the seedlings are produced they must eventually be moved into a soil mixture that is more nutrient-rich. However, a balance must be struck – particularly with the slower-growing species – or the young plants might still rot from exposure to too much richness and moisture.

▶ Rough and naturally textured pots, sculptures and enclosures interact quite attractively with cacti in nearly all settings.

◀ If planning to transplant round-sided cacti into containers, a good rule of thumb is to allow about 2 inches more in diameter than the width of the cactus itself.

◀ Many species of cacti occur naturally in rocky terrain and hobbyists often enjoy carrying that natural environment over into their cacti gardens.

CUTTINGS

Another very popular and easy method of propagation for many species of cacti is through cuttings. As a matter of fact, cuttings may be a better introduction to cacti propagation than seeds because of the faster results that can be achieved. Most species react very well to this method, the tools of which are a sharp knife, a pair of tweezers, some toothpicks and some rubber bands. Many of the clustering species will not even require a knife for the removal of their offshoots.

Mid-spring through summer is the optimum time of the year to use the cuttings method, although it is only during winter that the method should never be attempted. Of course this is not relevant for those readers in the warmer regions of the world, where cuttings will take hold at any time of the year.

Interesting displays can be created by encouraging species that grow into colony-like groupings.

METHODS OF PROPAGATION

BY SEED: A huge variety of seeds are available commercially through mail-order catalogues and retail outlets. Alternatively, they can be gathered from plants in the grower's collection. Although raising plants on a large scale takes a great deal of time and care, it is the best way for the novice to gain the skills required to raise different cacti. Two factors are crucial in seed germination: water and temperature. With this in mind, the following suggestions should prove useful: 1) use small containers, preferably plastic, that are shallow and can be covered by glass; 2) ensure that the seeds are freshly gathered or have been stored in airtight containers; 3) place seeds in indirect sunlight with plenty of warmth; 4) moisten the soil regularly, preferably by bottom soaking; and 5) sow the seeds in the spring to allow as long a "growing-on" time as possible.

BY CUTTINGS: A popular and easy method of propagation which produces fast results in most species. This method is easy to master, and the only tools required are a sharp knife, tweezers, toothpicks, and rubber bands. Most of the clustering species will not even require a knife to remove their offshoots. Midspring through summer is the best time to use the cuttings method, which simply involves taking an offshoot from the plant at its narrowest joint. The cutting should then be allowed to rest for a few days in a warm, dry place to allow the wound to heal before planting in a highly porous medium such as coarse sand, perlite or vermiculite.

BY GRAFTING: This is a very controversial method among many growers, producing "freaks" which can look very artificial. However, grafting achieves increased growth in slow-growing species, literally through grafting them onto speedier stock. The grafted specimen can then be removed once the desired growth has been achieved. Although more involved than the cuttings method, grafting is not a difficult process and all that is required is a sharp knife, toothpicks, and rubber bands. The two main methods are the *flat graft,* in which the cut surface of the graft and the stock plant are flat; and the *V-graft,* in which a V-shape is cut both into the stock plant and the graft, the latter being inserted upside down into the V-shape in the stock plant.

Cuttings should be taken at the most narrow joint you can find, which will shorten the needed drying period. While many other types of plants other than cacti can be propagated through cuttings immediately, with cacti the cutting should not be planted directly after being removed from the parent plant. More often than not, such a move will soon result in it rotting.

Instead, the cutting should be allowed to rest in a warm, dry place for several days (3–21) after it is taken. This allows a callus to form over the wound and prevents rotting. Cuttings that require longer drying periods will need to be turned over completely every few days to prevent their curling and bending.

I have never encountered any sort of chart to delineate the proper drying periods for different cacti cuttings. As a general rule, allow a longer drying period for those cuttings with large surface areas. Only your own experience over time will give a more specific idea of the timespans involved. In the meantime, take solace in the fact that few cacti will die from an overlong drying period.

Cuttings from many different species of cacti – particularly many of the easy-to-grow species that are most commonly available – will take root quite nicely and rather quickly in a growing medium, such as a commercially available cactus soil or in a highly porous medium such as coarse sand, perlite or vemiculite.

The cutting does not need a highly nutrient-rich growing medium at this point. The roots that it puts forth into the ground will be searching for water, and materials like sand, perlite and vermiculite will encourage and assist that probing search.

As with seeds, a good source of heat under the pot will help to hurry along the formation of roots in cuttings. But, unlike the seeds, a cutting needs sunlight to continue the food-producing process of photosynthesis. A sunny windowsill with a radiator beneath or nearby is a fine location for this purpose, as is a greenhouse. The direct rays of the sun, however, should be avoided and the cutting should be provided with shade.

After the cutting has sent out some roots and possibly even started to grow, it is time to transfer the new plant into the pot of growing medium where it will reside for the next few years.

PROPAGATION BY CUTTINGS

Slice through the stem with secateurs or a sharp knife

Put cuttings in a warm, dry place until a callus forms

Insert cuttings into compost, just deep enough to keep them upright

When cuttings show signs of growth, remove and pot them on

A large assortment of cacti may require a system of permanent labelling in order to differentiate among species that closely resemble one another.

Newcomers to the world of cacti are often amazed by the variety of forms that the plants take. Many of the *Rhipsalis* species, for example, more closely resemble vines or trees with hanging branches.

GRAFTING

There is one other means of creating a new cactus plant that is often frowned upon by the most dedicated enthusiasts. This other means is called grafting. However, while such specimens, particularly the orange-capped freaks widely available in supermarkets and department stores, can look very artificial, there are some good reasons in support of the practice of grafting.

One of the most compelling is the increased growth rate that can often be achieved in slow-growing species that have been grafted onto much faster growing stock. The 10–20 years that it takes some of the very slow-growing species to reach maturity can sometimes be cut by as much as half through grafting onto speedier stock. With the majority of cacti species it is possible – even easy – to remove the grafted specimen from the stock plant once the desired growth has been achieved. The grafted specimen can then be handled in a similar way to a cutting, i.e. by the technique described earlier.

Species of *Cereus*, *Echinopsis*, *Opuntia* and *Trichocereus* have been widely and successfully used as stock plants in the temperate regions of the North, while *Hylocereus* and *Myrtillocactus* species fulfil the function nicely in warmer, tropical regions.

Although it may seem to be much more involved, grafting is not a difficult process. A sharp knife, some toothpicks, and some rubber bands are all the tools that you will need.

The object in grafting is to join the vascular tissue of the graft to the vascular tissue of the stock plant. If you envisage the process that will occur between the two you will quickly see that there will be some shrinkage of these soft, liquidy vascular tissues during the ensuing period – and more shrinkage than will be seen in the much tougher exterior epidermis.

Because of these varying shrinkage rates, some additional epidermis will need to be trimmed away at the edges of the cut on both the graft and the stock plant, otherwise, the vascular tissues of both might shrink out of contact and be held apart by the epidermis which shrank less.

Of the two most widely used grafting methods, the *flat graft* is the simplest. As the name implies, both the cut surface of the graft and the cut surface of the stock plant are flat. To hold the graft in place, toothpicks can be placed into the stock plant around the edges of the graft, a rubber band can be stretched over the graft from toothpicks stuck into the sides of the stock plant, or a wire hoop can be placed over both the graft and the stock plant, rooted into the growing medium.

The other method is the *V-graft*, by which a V is cut into the stock plant to correspond to the inverted V shape cut into the base of the graft. The inverted V, or arrowhead, of the graft is inserted into the V of the stock plant. With the V-graft method, no additional means of holding the graft in place may be necessary.

With the actual grafting procedure completed, water the soil around the stock plant and place the whole affair in a warm, shaded location. It is important to keep the rays of the sun away from the graft area.

After two or three weeks – when new growth has begun to show on the graft – any restraint mechanism can be gently and carefully removed. Normal cacti-care procedures apply from this point forward with the exception that any natural offshoots produced by the stock plant should be removed immediately. (Leaving those offshoots in place on the plant generally will draw growth away from the graft, possibly to the point of killing it.)

REASONS FOR GRAFTING

Propagation Cacti that have difficulty growing from seed, cuttings or offsets often prosper by grafting

Weak roots Some cacti such as *Opuntia claveroides* have weak roots and need a stronger rootstock

No chlorophyll Coloured specimens such as the gymnocalycium "Black Cap" require a green rootstock

PICK YOUR OWN?

There is one other, very tempting, method of obtaining the cacti that you want. That is, of course, by taking them from the wild. I have just one word to relay on this subject: DON'T.

Our poor, old, beaten-up Earth simply has too many pressures placed on it already to allow this additional, needless attack. In many areas, man has already taxed the environment to the point that the loss of just a few plants could actually trigger a downward spiral and collapse of that environment.

Throughout much of the "cacti country" in the USA, state laws prohibit the removal of any wild plants. However, the existence of such laws and their enforcement are two very different subjects. As I write, much attention has been focused recently on the illegal removal of the stately "saguaro" from Saguaro National Monument in Arizona by poachers, who sell the big plants for as much as £25 per foot and £50 per branch. The extremely rare, crested specimens, of which there are probably less than 200 still in existence, are particularly at risk, selling for as much as £7,500 each.

Resource managers at the Monument have estimated that the *saguaro* population has dropped by as much as 75 percent since the mid-1930s in some parts of the "protected" zone. No amount of ornamentation in or around the home can be justified in the wake of such losses in the natural world.

Many species of cacti are much less threatened than these giants, but not to the extent that we should remove them from the wild – and there are plenty of sources available to us today so that we really don't need to act like the "great collectors" of a past age. In any case, the average enthusiast's chances of keeping the "captured" cacti alive in cultivation are slim at best.

▶ In clumping species, like these *Mammillaria gracilis*, each of the stems can be removed and planted on its own to produce a new plant.

Large-scale landscaping is quite possible in the right climes or for those who have other means of somehow protecting the warmth-loving plants during certain parts of the year.

SOIL

Whatever methods you employ to arrive at the cacti plants you obtain, you will need to make some decisions about the type of soil in which to grow them. Fortunately, this is one of the easier choices. Most species will do nicely in a wide range of soils; and the same species often does well in several different soil types in the wild.

The most important consideration though is how well the soil drains. This may seem a much simpler question than it really is. Drainage must be viewed in light of how quickly excess moisture leaves the soil and how hard the soil becomes when it dries. The perfect growing medium drains quickly but does not cake or clump when dry.

Although the adult cactus' nutrient needs are much less than most other types of domesticated plants, the cactus must still be able to satisfy its needs from the soil that you provide. A soil that is one part well-rotted leaf mould (not sterilized) to one part sterilized, coarse sand seems to help most cacti species perform beautifully. If you've selected a pot size appropriate for the size that the cactus should grow into over the next two or three years, filling it with this mixture should give the plant all the nutrients it needs for that period.

A richer soil-mix can be obtained by adding a second equal part of leaf mould and small amounts of bone meal, gypsum and phosphate, although these won't really be necessary. Of course, an infrequent addition of soluble fertilizer to the regular watering of the plant won't damage it – as long as such supplements are added infrequently.

If you are growing your cacti in plastic pots rather than clay, you may want to lean ever so slightly to the coarse sand side of the mixture, especially for slower-growing species. This can offset the ability of plastic pots to hold water much longer than clay pots – a factor that might even be desirable in warmer, more humid climates.

SOIL MIXES

A bewildering variety of soil types and climates make up the natural habitat of the cactus, and amply demonstrate the excellent adaptability of this plant. It is mostly found in the area running from the Canadian border of North America through Central America and the West Indies into South America, and as far south as Argentina and Brazil. Within this area alone cacti species thrive in true desert environments (with less than 10 inches of rain per year); in desert grasslands (arid to semi-arid regions bordering on desert); in low bushlands or chaparrals (typified by greater depth of soil, nearly complete bush cover, more rain and less drastic temperatures than in the desert regions, as the bush cover protects more sensitive species from the rays of the sun and allows them to flourish); and, finally, in subtropical forests (warm, humid regions with nutrient-rich soils where numerous epiphytic and climbing cacti grow).

Although the grower can obtain soil mixes for all his or her cacti species' requirements, in general these soil mixes should have the following properties in common: good drainage abilities, a coarse texture to allow for ease of penetration, small amounts of nitrogen, and an overall balance of nutrients.

A complete range of soil mixes are available from most stockists, but the three main types are as follows:

FINE: One part crushed gravel to two parts sieved peat compost. The mixture is nutrient-rich and requires no fertilizer; it is usually sterilized. Suitable for seedlings and young plants.

MEDIUM COARSE: A mix of 30 per cent peat, 30 per cent sieved garden soil, and 40 per cent coarse gravel. Suitable for taller, vigorously growing cacti such as *Lobivia* and *Opuntia,* and for plants with a stout tap-root such as *Copiapoa*. A humus-enriched mix increases moisture retention and is good for tropical types such as *Zygocactus*. For such a mix, halve the quantity of coarse gravel and add 20 per cent peat moss.

COARSE: A mix of 50 per cent coarse gravel, 25 per cent peat, and 25 per cent roughly sieved compost. This mix allows for rapid drainage and is suitable for all spherical Mexican or American desert cacti.

Many people select cacti for their homes because of the plant's legendary ability to withstand long periods without water, i.e. they require little attention!

WATERING

Watering of cacti should always be done from over the top of the plant, with only a few exceptions (notably when grafting is being done or when the cactus is in flower). At other times, overhead watering will help to keep the cactus clean and free of pests. A good dousing should be carried out every month to month-and-a-half during the entire growing period from spring to mid-autumn.

Determining the correct times to water is one area in which clay pots have the advantage over plastic. A look at the underside of a clay pot generally reveals the condition of water in the soil. If the underside is dry and the soil is dry to the depth of about an inch, it is probably time to water the clay-potted cactus. You'll have to rely on the finger-probe method alone with plastic pots.

Self-watering pots, in which a bottom reservoir is filled with water and continues to service the soil in the pot over an extended period, are not generally recommended for cacti. Gardeners who use such devices tend to overlook the importance of overhead watering in cacti culture.

Bowl gardens consisting of various cacti species also present some severe watering problems. Unless the species have been very carefully selected for compatibility in growth rates and water needs, the chances are that not all of the specimens are going to survive for very long.

One further watering consideration is the quality of the water itself. The chemicals added to many municipal water suplies can lead to problems in all plants – and not only cacti – such as brown areas on them or dead and shrivelled sections. If at all possible it is advisable to use distilled water, bottled spring water or collected rainwater to avoid the chemicals present in your home's water supply. Out of curiosity, you may also want to have a sample of your area's water tested to see exactly what chemicals you are getting in your water. In these days of pollution concerns, there are laboratories that carry out such testing.

HUMIDITY AND SUNSHINE

Humidity is another concern when growing cacti in the home. However, in this respect, today's home is well equipped indeed. With modern heating methods and insulation capabilities, our homes generally have incredibly low levels of humidity. This is fine for most species of cacti, although it is not so healthy for many other types of plants common to the home.

Most species of cacti when growing indoors need to be located in a sunny spot, particularly during the heavy growth period from spring through early autumn. If you cannot avoid growing your cacti in a shaded spot, cut back on watering so that the plant's development does not occur at its normal rate, otherwise the growth will be very delicate and spindly.

On the other hand, indoor cacti in a sunny location must be turned completely around, gradually, over the course of each week, otherwise the cacti will react like any indoor plant, producing a definite growth toward the sun. This can become particularly pronounced with a number of the taller, columnar species.

Many of the cacti being offered at various retail outlets are of this taller type. These are generally easy to grow in large quantities, and are hardy and strong for growing in the home. However, if flowers are part of your plans these are not the best choices. Generally they won't produce flowers until they reach heights of 6–10 feet, which is several years off even at their fast growth rates. Some of these cacti are in the genera of *Cephalocereus, Cereus, Lophocereus, Opuntia, Pachycereus* and *Trichocereus*.

Some less commonly available species – usually only available from specialist cacti suppliers – are slower growing but will give you flowers much sooner and are better suited to indoor growth. Some of the genera to consider for this are: *Chamaecereus, Coryphantha, Echinocereus, Echinopsis, Lobivia, Mammillaria, Melocactus, Notocactus, Parodia* and *Rebutia*.

▲
At its best, the growing
of cacti creates a new
type of environment in
and around the home.

COMMON PESTS

Adult red spider mite – under 1/24 of an inch in size – straw-coloured and turning red when faced with starvation.

Adult aphid – approximately 1/8 of an inch in size. Damages plants by puncturing flower buds and young tissues near the growing tips with its pointed "beak".

Adult white fly – reaches 1/8 of an inch in size. Damage to plants results from its oval-shaped larvae.

Adult, female mealy bug – approximately 1/24 of an inch in size – without the antennae and wings of the male. Colonies of these insects protect themselves with a cotton-wool-like coverage, which is excreted by the female.

PESTS

With cacti, pests are not nearly the problem that they are with many other types of domesticated plants. Cacti have a much more formidable line of defence in the tough epidermal layer that covers their surface. In addition, cacti are generally grown indoors or under much more tightly controlled conditions outdoors, giving pests less of an opportunity to gain a foothold.

Direct attack on any pests that do surface damage should be the gardener's first priority. If you are tending your plants daily you should notice any change in them at an early stage. Given such advance warning, the gardener may well have the opportunity to simply pluck the offenders off or to flush them away with a blast of water.

For more severe infestations you may need to turn to insecticides. Avoid the systemic types, as these remain active and toxic within the plants for several weeks after application. Too potent a dose, sometimes even within the stated guidelines, can kill particularly sick or young plants. If the systemics seem to be your only choice, plan to quarantine the sick plant for several weeks, particularly where children or pets are concerned.

Among the most common cacti pests are mealy bugs, red spider mites and the various scale insects. Although mealy bugs may be present in the soil of your pots for several months before showing themselves, the first you will probably learn of their presence is when tiny areas of cotton-like material appear on the plants. A small insect will be found under each cottony patch. These adult insects can be removed from the plant with a solution of soapy water applied directly to them with a small paintbrush. However, you can expect future outbreaks because this will not kill the eggs in the soil. Repotting might be advisable at this time.

Anyone who has been around any type of houseplant, cacti included, for even the most limited amount of time, probably knows what the red spider mite looks like. It is a highly destructive pest, the damage usually first appearing in the form of browning plant tips. Overhead watering is both the preventative and the cure for these creatures.

Scale insects appear to be very small marine limpets affixed to the surface of the infected plant. The destructiveness of these pests lies in the rabbit-like speed with which they multiply. Within just a few months an untreated plant will be completely covered by them, each drawing a tiny bit of nourishment out of the plant. If only a few scale insects are present they can be removed with a solution of soapy water. More chemically oriented treatments are often necessary for wider infestations.

OUTDOOR GARDENING

Many more pests will attack those cacti that you plant outdoors, but the unusual landscaping possibilities more than offset such problems for many gardeners. Exactly which species can be planted around your home will, of course, depend largely on where in the world you live. A hot, dry climate can obviously support the widest possible range of species – provided a certain amount of shading is given to some of the more sun-delicate species.

In planning your outdoor cacti garden, the first move is to become acquainted with the past weather trends for your area. The winter season is of most concern. Cold and dry will suit most cacti admirably. But if most of the annual rainfall arrives during a cold period, you may have to enhance the natural drainage abilities of your site so that the cacti are not standing in too much water at a time of the year when they cannot use it for growth.

Also, give some thought to the sunlight that will be falling on the site. While many species of cacti will flourish in fairly full sunlight, once they've reached adulthood, there are also many that require partial to full shading from the sun, and many others again that need shade to begin life. The giant *saguaro* cactus of the American Southwest, for example, spends the first few years of its life in the shade of the Palo Verde tree. As the cactus' root system spreads out, it eventually starves the tree of moisture. The Palo Verde gradually dies, leaving only the cactus, which is now ready to face the rays of the sun directly.

In addition, the epidermis of cactus that you have just purchased will be significantly more sensitive to *all* ele-

ments, including the sun. It will need a period of hardening off, as it is gradually introduced to the vagaries of the outdoors, including shade from the direct rays of the sun and, sometimes, shelter from strong, cold winds.

With this basic course in cactus husbandry behind you, you are ready to begin considering some selections for your own growing efforts. What follows is a directory of 150 of the most commonly available, and yet widely diverse, species of cacti, each with detailed information on its life history and growing needs. All entries are pretty much self-explanatory.

Included in the directory are the common names for a few of the species. For most of the entries, however, these are missing. Only a relatively limited number of such names will be recognized beyond certain regions or certain groups of cacti enthusiasts. For this reason, you will generally be more successful in communicating and learning about cacti if you use the scientific names.

Now, let us begin an exciting journey . . .

▼

In more northerly climes, the combination of cold and wet weather makes an outdoor cacti garden a risky proposition. In these circumstances, it is normally important that your plants are potted and can easily be transported into the home.

IMPERIAL TO METRIC CONVERSION TABLE			
Inches to mm		**Feet to Meters**	
⅛	3	1	0.3
¼	6	2	0.6
⅜	10	3	0.9
½	13	4	1.2
⅝	16	5	1.5
¾	19	6	1.8
⅞	22	7	2.1
		8	2.4
		9	2.7
Inches to mm		10	3.0
1	2.5	15	4.6
2	5	20	6.1
3	7.5	25	7.6
4	10	30	9.1
5	12.5	35	10.7
6	15	40	12.2
7	18	45	13.7
8	20.5	50	15.2
9	23	55	16.8
10	25.5	60	18.3
11	28		

Shape

This symbol represents the basic shape the cactus will make when grown in a pot.

Columnar   Clustering

Globular   Leaf-like

Padded/jointed   Pendent

Sprawling/trailing   Climbing

Flowering time

DAY-FLOWERING

By far the greatest number of cacti are diurnal, or day-flowering. This symbol indicates that the flowers of a particular species are only to be found fully open during daylight hours. Where flowers last for a number of days, they may remain open day and night throughout the period, or close towards evening, then re-open the next morning.

NIGHT-FLOWERING

This symbol applies to nocturnal, or night-flowering cacti. These tend to be mainly the columnar plants, particularly those from South American habitats. However, nocturnal flowers also occur on a number of globular plants. The flower buds are tightly closed during the hours of daylight, and commence opening in the late afternoon or early evening, or even during night hours. With the majority of species, the flowers remain open throughout the hours of darkness and begin to close again in early morning. In some cases the blooms last for one night only.

INFORMATION UNKNOWN

This symbol is used when the information is unknown.

Flowering period

These symbols give a general indication as to when a particular plant should bloom. Sometimes nature decides to vary the flowering season of a plant slightly, but such variation will be minimal. There is also the possibility of a second flowering season occurring later in the same year, but this phenomenon is a more rare event!

Mid-winter   Mid-spring

Mid-summer   Mid-fall

Late winter to early spring   Late spring to early summer

Late summer to early fall   Late fall to early winter

Light

GOOD BUT INDIRECT LIGHT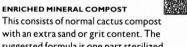

A large number of cacti appreciate brief periods of bright sunshine, but not throughout the heat of the day. Place these plants in a position where there is plenty of indirect or filtered light, but not too much shade. In a hot, sunny summer, greenhouse specimens may need protection from scorching. Greenhouse shading can be provided either by using blinds, or by coating the glass with a special substance called "summer cloud", which provides a thin coating of white that moderates the intensity of the light. On the approach of fall this should be wiped off.

PARTIAL SHADE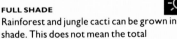

In the wild, many cacti, especially the smaller species, grow in the protective shade of surrounding desert bushes and scrub. Such plants appreciate semi-shade, even in northern climes, and require protection from the full glare of the midday sun. Indoors, place these plants on a window ledge that does not receive direct sunlight. In the greenhouse, use blinds or other forms of shading to filter out some of the light. Cacti planted in the garden will appreciate the shade provided by overhanging tree branches or a nearby wall.

FULL SHADE

Rainforest and jungle cacti can be grown in shade. This does not mean the total exclusion of light, but these species do best in a position where the light is finely shaded at all times. Many such plants are grown "under the bench" in greenhouses; in the home, they can be stood in windows which do not get too much sunlight, or brought away from the window altogether.

DIRECT SUNLIGHT

Some cactus species can withstand extended periods of full sun without coming to any harm. Plants grown indoors should be placed on a bright, sunny window ledge; in a greenhouse, place them as near to the glass as possible; in the garden, choose a sheltered, sunny aspect.

Compost

SLIGHTLY ACID COMPOST

The basic mixture consists of equal parts sterilized loam, shredded peat and coarse washed sand, or sand and perlite. To achieve the required acidity, mix a small quantity of thoroughly decomposed leaf mold or cow manure in granulated form with the peat: about one quarter in bulk of the peat content is sufficient. Suitable for forest cacti such as *Disocactus*, *Rhipsalis*, *Schumbergera* and so on.

PROPRIETARY CACTUS COMPOST

This is the type of compost invariably offered commercially for cactus and succulent plant culture. Normally composed of equal parts sterilized loam, shredded sphagnum peat and sharp gritty sand, to which is added a slow-release base fertilizer. If a soil-less compost is considered, add one part coarse washed sand to three parts compost to increase porosity and aid drainage.

ENRICHED MINERAL COMPOST

This consists of normal cactus compost with an extra sand or grit content. The suggested formula is one part sterilized loam, one part shredded peat, and two parts sharp gritty sand or fine gravel, enriched with thoroughly decomposed leaf mold in granulated form at the rate of three parts prepared compost to one part leaf mold. Suitable for cacti from rocky, sloping habitats, where decomposed leaves from the surrounding scrub and low trees, plus minerals washed from the rocks, provide the necessary nutrients.

CALCAREOUS COMPOST

This consists of normal cactus compost with the addition of limestone gravel or chippings (never powdered lime or chalk). The quantity of limestone added depends on the species concerned, but in general one part limestone gravel to six parts compost is sufficient. Suitable for the spiny or woolly type of desert cacti. The addition of limestone assists in strong spine formation.

Temperature

The temperatures stated pertain to night-time conditions, and are recommended as a *minimum* for the well-being of the plant.

45°F   59–61°F

50°F   64°F

55°F   66°F and over

A-Z of Cacti Species

Acanthocalycium thionanthum

▼

tribe
Cacteae

subtribe
Echinocereinae

description
Spherical to somewhat cylindrical, 2¼–4 inches in diameter, maximum 5 inches tall, about 14 ribs. It has areoles at the apex of the tubercles, is covered at the base with brown to grey felt, and the upper part curves around the sides of the rib. There are as many as 10 radial spines and 4 central spines, each about ¾ of an inch, and brown to pale yellow in colour. Flowers are about 2 inches long with a hairy tube, and brownish to bright yellow.

origin
Argentina

cultivation
The minimum temperature for the adult plant is 50°F (10°C). It is best propagated through cuttings.

flowering period
Mid-summer

Acanthocalycium violaceum

▲

tribe
Cacteae

subtribe
Echinocereinae

description
Globular to slightly columnar, green, about 5 inches in diameter and as much as 8 inches tall. There are about 15 ribs. Areoles are covered with off-white felt and have 12 or more thin, tan, radial spines and 3 or 4 slightly longer central spines. The flowers are pale pink, bell-shaped, about 2½ inches in diameter and 3 inches long. They grow from or near the apex.

origin
Argentina

cultivation
The minimum temperature for the adult plant is 50°F (10°C). It cannot tolerate much lower temperatures. The plant needs full sunlight and a well-ventilated location. It is propagated through seeds.

flowering period
Summer

Ancistrocactus crassihamatus

▲

tribe
Cacteae

subtribe
Echinocactinae

description
Globular, olive-green, from 4–6 inches
in diameter. There are 12–14 protruding
ribs, heavily notched horizontally. The
widely scattered areoles are covered with
greyish felt. They each have 7 or 8, thick
and flattened, greenish-grey, radial
spines, and as many as 5 reddish central
spines that can be as long as 2½ inches,
one of which will be hooked at the tip.
The flowers are purple, tubular, and
about ¾ of an inch long. They appear
near the apex.

origin
Mexico

cultivation
The minimum temperature for the adult
plant is 50°F (10°C). The plant needs
full sunlight and must have protection
from lower temperatures. It is
propagated through seeds or cuttings.

flowering period
Summer

Ancistrocactus tobuschii

▼

tribe
Cacteae

subtribe
Echinocactinae

description
Globular, dark olive-green, about
3 inches in diameter. The protruding
tubercles are arranged in a spiral around
the stem, each one tipped by an areole
covered with white felt. They have as
many as 7, thin, white, 1–2-inch-long,
radial spines and 3, inch-long, central
spines. The flowers are tubular, about
1½ inches long, and yellow.

origin
Texas, USA

cultivation
The minimum temperature for the adult
plant is 50°F (10°C). It needs partial
shading from the direct rays of
the summer sun. It is propagated
through seeds.

flowering period
Summer

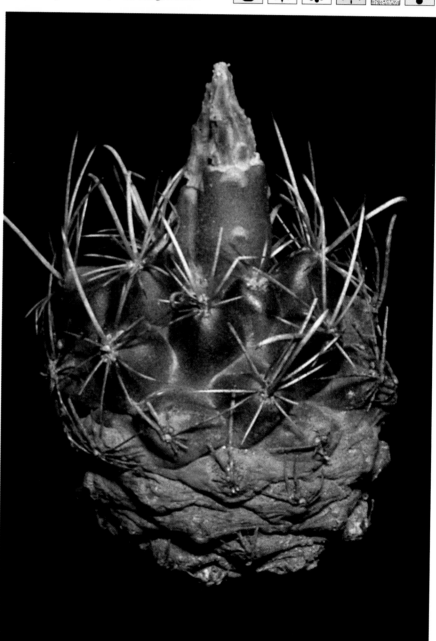

Ancistrocactus uncinatus

tribe
Cacteae

subtribe
Echinocactinae

description
Columnar with a flattened apex, pale
blue-green, about 3 inches in diameter
and as tall as 8 inches. There are as many
as 13 protruding, straight ribs, bulging at
the areoles. The latter are covered with
white felt and also have pale yellow
hairs. They each have about 8, thick,
white, radial spines and 1 or 2, similar,
central spines, one of which is hooked at
the tip. The flowers are bell-shaped,
about 1 inch long, and burnt orange with
white edges on the petals. They grow
from the apex.

origin
Texas and Mexico

cultivation
The minimum temperature for the adult
plant is 50°F (10°C). The plant needs
direct sunlight and a soil that carries a
good amount of grit. It is propagated
through seeds.

flowering period
Mid-summer

Aporocactus martianus

tribe
Cacteae

subtribe
Hylocereinae

description
Prostate-creeping or hanging columnar,
with many stems, each about ¾ of an
inch in diameter and more than 3 feet in
length. Each has 8 protruding ribs. The
cream-coloured, felt-covered areoles are
spaced from ¼–½ an inch along the
ribs. Each one has 6–8 thin, yellowish,
radial spines and 2 or more central spines
that are also yellowish but bristly in
appearance. The flowers are bell-shaped,
about 2½ inches in diameter and
4 inches long, and are bright red.
They grow along the stems.

origin
Mexico

cultivation
The minimum temperature for the adult
plant is 55°F (13°C). The plant cannot
tolerate lower temperatures than this and
needs direct sunlight throughout the
year. It is propagated through
cuttings or seeds.

flowering period
Early summer

Aporocactus flagelliformis
(RAT-TAIL CACTUS)

◄

tribe
Cacteae

subtribe
Hylocereinae

description
Rounded, creeping or hanging stems,
about ¾ of an inch in diameter and as
long as 7 feet, with 10–14 very slight
ribs. The areoles are very close, with
10–15 radial spines, about ¼ of an inch
long, and reddish to yellowish brown.
There are also 3–4 central spines with
yellow tips. The flowers are about
3 inches long, bright pink with
yellow filaments.

origin
Mexico

cultivation
The minimum temperature for the adult
plant is 50°F (10°C). It is propagated
through cuttings during the summer.
The plant needs a rest period,
full sunlight and ample water
during the summer.

flowering period
Late spring

A

Ariocarpus kotschoubeyanus
(LIVING ROCK CACTUS)

▼

tribe
Cacteae

subtribe
Echinocactinae

description
Concentric circles of grey-green,
triangular tubercles with grey-white felt
at their bases and through a middle
"part", each about ½ an inch thick at
base. The flowers are about 1¼ inches in
diameter with white hair at the base, and
are brown on outer segments and pink
to red on inner ones.

origin
Mexico

cultivation
The minimum temperature for the adult
plant is 50°F (10°C). It is propagated
from shoots taken from adult plants, and
needs plenty of sunlight and adequate
space for the roots. It is a very
slow grower.

flowering period
Spring or autumn

Ariocarpus retusus
(SEVEN STARS)

▲

tribe
Cacteae

subtribe
Echinocactinae

description
Flattened globular, pale greyish-green,
as much as 10 inches in diameter.
Its tubercles are teardrop-shaped, about
¾ of an inch long, flattened but
pointing upward, with a golden tip.
The flowers are tubular, about 1½
inches long, and pale pink with some
white. They grow from the apex.

origin
Mexico

cultivation
The minimum temperature for the adult
plant is 50°F (10°C). The plant needs
direct sunlight, a soil that is well-drained
but rich, and regular but careful
watering. It is propagated through
seeds or cuttings.

flowering period
Summer

Ariocarpus scapharostrus

tribe
Cacteae

subtribe
Echinocactinae

description
Globular, olive-green, about 3½ inches in diameter. Its tubercles are triangular, upward pointing, blunt at the tip, and about 2 inches long. The base of the tubercles are covered with a greyish-white felt. The plant does not have aeroles or spines. Its flowers are bell-shaped, about 1½ inches in diameter, with bright (almost neon) purplish-red petals and equally bright yellow stamens. They grow from the centre of the plant and extend beyond the tubercles.

origin
Mexico

cultivation
The minimum temperature for the adult plant is 55°F (13°C). The plant needs direct sunlight and a well-drained, gritty soil. It should be kept dry throughout the winter. It is propagated through cuttings or seeds.

flowering period
Summer

Arrojadoa rhodantha

tribe
Cacteae

subtribe
Cereinae

description
Rounded and erect stem, flattened at the top, ¾–2 inches in diameter and up to 6 feet in length, with 10–12 slight ribs. The stem often branches at its base. Its areoles are about ½ an inch apart with light brown felt at the base, 20–50 thin, brown, radial spines, and 5–7 central spines which are longer and thicker. The stem and each branch has a soft, hair-like tuft of brown and white at the end. Its flowers are about 1½ inches long, tubular, and red in colour. The fruit is round and purple.

origin
Brazil

cultivation
The minimum temperature for the adult plant is 55°F (13°C). It is propagated from cuttings, and needs semi-shade conditions and a soil consisting of humus, sand and small stones.

flowering period
Early summer

Astrophytum asterias
(SEA URCHIN CACTUS)

tribe
Cacteae

subtribe
Echinocactinae

description
Globular but distinctly flattened across the apex, green-speckled throughout with roundish white scales, about 4 inches in diameter and 2 inches tall. There are 8 slightly raised and rounded ribs, each with a centred row of white felt-covered protruding areoles, spaced about ¼ of an inch apart. The areoles have a yellowish tint at the apex, where there is a central area of greyish felt.

The cactus has no spines. Its flowers are about 1¼ inches long, and about 2 inches in diameter with yellowish petals, slightly reddish in the throat. They grow near the apex.

origin
Texas and Mexico

cultivation
The minimum temperature for the adult plant is 45°F (7°C). The plant needs full sunlight throughout the summer and constantly warm temperatures throughout the winter. It is propagated through seeds.

flowering period
Summer

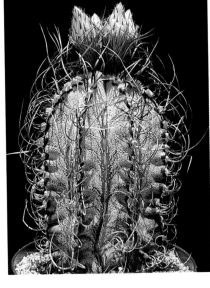

Astrophytum capricorne
(GOAT-HORN CACTUS)

tribe
Cacteae

subtribe
Echinocactinae

description
Globular to cylindrical stem, green covered with white scales, as tall as 8 inches, 8 or 9 pronounced ribs. The areoles are about 1 inch apart, and covered with grey-brown felt, each with as many as 10 upward-curved, dark brown spines, about 2¾ inches long. The plant has red to orange flowers, and its fruit is red, elliptical and spiny with limited felt.

origin
Mexico

cultivation
The minimum temperature for the adult plant is 50°F (10°C). It is propagated through seeds, and needs direct sunlight and a rest period during the winter at a temperature near freezing point.

flowering period
Several times during summer

Astrophytum myriostigma
(BISHOP'S CAP)

tribe
Cacteae

subtribe
Echinocactinae

description
Globular to cylindrical with 3–8, very pronounced ribs, green with many tiny white scales across the surface. The areoles are very close together, some touching; it has no spines but is covered with grey-brown felt. The flowers are about 2½ inches in diameter, and yellow to orange in colour.

origin
Mexico

cultivation
The minimum temperature for the adult plant is 50°F (10°C). It is propagated through seeds or shoots from old plants, and needs full sunlight and well-drained soil.

flowering period
Summer

Astrophytum ornatum
(STAR CACTUS)

tribe
Cacteae

subtribe
Echinocactinae

description
Columnar, green stem with feather-like areas of white scales, as much as 12 inches in diameter and up to 6 feet tall, 8 sharp ribs. The areoles are about ½ an inch apart, with bands of 5–11 stiff, brown spines. Its flowers are about 3 inches in diameter, and light yellow in colour. Its fruit is oval with felt and spines, and red in colour.

origin
Mexico

cultivation
The minimum temperature for the adult plant is 50°F (10°C). It is propagated through seeds, and needs full sunlight and porous, well-drained soil.

flowering period
Summer to autumn

Austrocephalocereus dybowskii

tribe
Cacteae

subtribe
Cereinae

description
Several felt-covered stems, each about 3 inches in diameter grow straight upwards from the base, some reaching heights of as much as 13 feet. As many as 20 slight ribs with close-set areoles may run along a stem. The short, radial spines are mostly hidden beneath the felt, while 2 or 3 central spines protrude outwards. These yellowish-brown central spines are readily viewed. The cephalium can extend as much as 24 inches down along the stem from the apex. Its flowers are about 1½ inches long, bell-shaped, with segments on the petals, and white. They are nocturnal.

origin
Brazil

cultivation
The minimum temperature for the adult plant is 59°F (15°C). It needs full sunlight from spring through to early autumn, and a protected location for the rest of the year. It is propagated through cuttings.

flowering period
Summer

Aztekium ritteri
▼

tribe
Cacteae

subtribe
Echinocactinae

description
Globular, depressed, lime-green, about 2 inches in diameter. There are about 10 rounded ribs protruding noticeably, with much smaller protrusions between them. The entire stem is circled horizontally by irregular indentation lines, which fan out more from top to bottom, giving the appearance of scaling. The close-set areoles are covered by white felt and have a few very short spines. Its flowers are about ½ an inch wide, growing at the apex, and are white with light pink edges.

origin
Mexico

cultivation
The minimum temperature for the adult plant is 50°F (10°C). The plant needs full sunlight, with complete protection from colder temperatures. It performs best when grown in sandy soil, and is propagated through cuttings.

flowering period
Summer

Backebergia militaris
▲

tribe
Cacteae

subtribe
Cereinae

description
Columnar, branching into an almost tree-like canopy, as much as 20 feet tall, with stems that measure as much as 5 inches in diameter. There are 5–12 slightly protruding ribs. The areoles are covered with off-white felt, and have 7–13, grey-white, radial spines and as many as 4, slightly longer (about ½ an inch), grey-white, central spines. The apex of the stem is covered by a crown of burnt orange hairs. The bell-shaped, silky white flowers grow from this cephalium. They are about 1½ inches in diameter and 3 inches long, and they bloom at night.

origin
Mexico

cultivation
The minimum temperature for the adult plant is 55°F (13°C). The plant needs direct sunlight. It is propagated through cuttings and seeds.

flowering period
Summer

Borzicactus roezlii

▼

tribe
Cacteae

subtribe
Cereinae

description
Elongated stem with rounded apex, green flecked with grey-white, about 1½ inches in diameter and as much as 5 feet tall; additional stems may shoot from the base. There are about 10 vertical ribs, connected by V-shaped subribs, giving the appearance of total segmentation. White felt-covered aeroles appear on the most protruding portion of each segment. Eight or more brown to grey radial spines are about ½ an inch long each. One or 2 of the central spines are similar, but slightly longer – by as much as ¾ of an inch. The spines near the apex are reddish-brown. Its flowers are about 1½ inches long, growing at the curve of the apex, with tubes covered by hair and scales; the outer petals are red, the inner petals are pink.

origin
Ecuador

cultivation
The minimum temperature for the adult plant is 55°F (13°C). The plant needs full sunlight during the summer, and is propagated through cuttings.

flowering period
Summer

Borzicactus samaipatanus

▲

tribe
Cacteae

subtribe
Cereinae

description
Vertical stems branch from the base, yellowish-green, no more than 1½ inches in diameter but as much as 5 feet tall. An even number of ribs, 14 or 16, are evenly spaced around the stem. The aeroles are reddish-brown, spaced about ¼ of an inch apart and staggered with those on the adjacent ribs. Spines are grey- to yellow-brown with reddish tips, ranging from ⅛–1¼ inches in length. The flowers grow around the edge of the apex curve, extending nearly horizontally. They are many shades of red, with lighter stamens and lemon-yellow stigma. The flower tube is covered with hair and scales. The fruit is red and round, and covered with felt.

origin
Bolivia

cultivation
The minimum temperature for the adult plant is 50°F (10°C) – and a bit colder if the soil is dry. It needs moderate to full sunlight, and performs best in sandy, but moist soil. It is propagated through seeds or cuttings.

flowering period
Summer

C

Browningia hertlingiana

tribe
Cacteae

subtribe
Cereinae

description
Columnar with a rounded apex, sky or milky blue, as much as 1 foot in diameter and as tall as 26 feet. There are 18 ribs, bulging at the areoles with wedge-shaped indentations between the areoles. There is only a light covering of white felt across the areoles. From 4–30 yellow to brown radial spines grow from the areole, with more mature areas of the plant having a larger number of spines, and 1–3 longer central spines. The spines of areoles near the apex are much more rigid than across the rest of the plant. With maturity most stems tend to branch. Flowers are about 2 inches in diameter, tubular with an upward curve, reddish-brown, with many scales along the tube.

origin
Peru

cultivation
The minimum temperature for the adult plant is 55°F (13°C). It is still a rare species in cultivation, although this condition is changing. It is propagated through cuttings or seeds.

flowering period
Summer

Carnegiea gigantea
(SAGUARO)

tribe
Cacteae

subtribe
Cereinae

description
This is the typical western-movie cactus and probably the most familiar of all cacti. It has an elongated stem, brownish-green, branching at about 7 feet and repeatedly beyond that point, both from main stem and from branches. The plant has been reported to reach a height of 60 feet with a main stem of more than 2 feet in diameter. One or two dozen ribs run vertically along each stem. Its areoles are spaced at about ¾ of an inch intervals, and closer near the apex of each stem, with 3–6 central spines of as much as 2¾ inches each. The spines are brown to brown-grey. Its flowers are about 4½ inches wide and long, appearing on the upper reaches of any of the stems, and they are white with a light green tube. The fruit is red and eliptical.

origin
Southwestern USA

cultivation
The minimum temperature for the adult plant is 50°F (10°C). It is very slow growing: 1 foot in 10 years is typical. The plant needs full sunlight, and is propagated through seeds.

flowering period
Spring

Cephalocereus hoppenstedtii
▼

tribe
Cacteae

subtribe
Cereinae

description
Columnar, grey-green, about 1 foot in diameter and as much as 33 feet tall. The plant does not branch, but it does grow in small, loose groupings. There are about 16 ribs that bear close-set areoles, which are covered with off-white felt. Each areole has 12–18, off-white, ½-an-inch-long, radial spines and 4–8, off-white, ¾-of-an-inch-long, central spines. A pseudocephalium of grey-white wool and yellowish spines grows near the apex. From this growth, the tubular, pale yellow flowers sprout. They are nocturnal bloomers.

origin
Mexico

cultivation
The minimum temperature for the adult plant is 55°F (13°C). The plant needs direct sunlight and a soil that has a high limestone content. It is propagated through seeds or cuttings.

flowering period
Summer

Cephalocereus senilis
(OLD-MAN CACTUS)
▲

tribe
Cacteae

subtribe
Cereinae

description
Usually a single elongated stem, curved at the apex, green but covered with blue-grey hair in the upper reaches, as much as 1 foot 4 inches in diameter and up to 50 feet tall. The stem has 12–15 ribs in young plants and as many as 30 ribs in mature plants. Its close-set areoles have as many as 5 pale-yellow spines and up to 30 off-white bristles. The flowers are night-blooming, borne along one side of the stem near the apex, and about 3 inches in diameter, with pink outer petals and cream stamens. Its fruit is red and covered with cream hairs.

origin
Mexico

cultivation
The minimum temperature for the adult plant is 55°F (13°C). It needs moderate to full sunlight, and is propagated through seeds.

flowering period
Spring

C

Cleistocactus jujuyensis

tribe
Cacteae

subtribe
Cactinae

description
Globular, when young, to columnar with a rounded apex, dark blue-green, about 1½ inches in diameter and as long as 6½ feet. The stem begins life in an erect posture, but eventually becomes drooping. It branches profusely from its central root. The stem is divided into slightly raised, cone-shaped tubercles, each with a white felt-covered areole. The areoles appear to be arranged in a spiral around the stem. Six to 10, yellow to grey, radial spines, about ½ an inch long, and one white central spine with a hooked tip, about 1¼ inches long, grow from the areole. Its flowers are about 1¼ inches long, tubular with outward curling petals and protruding stamens and pistil, all glossy red.

origin
Mexico

cultivation
The minimum temperature for the adult plant is 50°F (10°C). The plant needs full sunlight and a distinct rest period during the winter. It is propagated through cuttings.

flowering period
Summer

Cereus peruvianus

▲

tribe
Cacteae

subtribe
Cereinae

description
Columnar, with branches, bright blue-green about 4 inches to 1 foot in diameter and 9–15 feet tall. There are 5–8 protruding ribs that are notched where the areoles appear (about every ¾ of an inch), with deep furrows between the ribs. Each areole is covered with tan felt and has 4–8 golden, ½-an-inch-long, radial spines and one, reddish, ¾-of-an-inch-long, central spine. The flowers are tubular, about 6 inches long, with white inside petals and brown outside petals. They are nocturnal.

origin
Argentina

cultivation
The minimum temperature for the adult plant is 50°F (10°C). It needs full sunlight, and is propagated through seeds or cuttings.

flowering period
Summer

C

Copiapoa cinerea
▼

tribe
Cacteae

subtribe
Echinocactinae

description
Younger plants are globular, but become more columnar with maturity, growing to a diameter of 3–5 inches and a height of as much as 3 feet 4 inches. The stem is chalk-white with about 18–24 ribs, divided horizontally as well by substantial depressions cutting between the tubercles. The apex is curved, often slightly concave, with a noticeably different cream colouring to it. Its centre also lacks the segmentation of the rest of the stem. The areoles are covered with white felt. Varying with different types, there may be just one central spine or as many as 8 radial and 2 central spines. In mature plants the spines are dark purple to black. Additional stems may emerge from the base. Flowers are funnel-shaped, about 1 inch long, with yellow to orange petals and a light yellow tube with a red-tinted tip. The fruit is round and orange.

origin
Chile

cultivation
The minimum temperature for the adult plant is 50°F (10°C). Full sunlight is needed, as is a well-drained soil. It is propagated through seeds. Surprising results may emerge in new plants, because the plant occurs as a wide range of naturally occurring hybrids.

flowering period
Summer

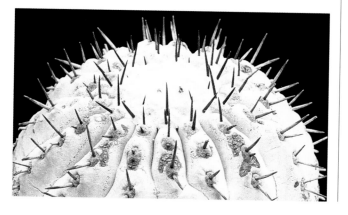

Copiapoa hypogaea
▲

tribe
Cacteae

subtribe
Echinocactinae

description
Globular with a rounded apex, dull brown, about 2–3 inches in diameter, with a very rough surface. There are 10–12 protruding ribs arranged spirally around the stem, deeply divided into tubercles. The apex of the plant has a growth of white wool, and a white wool-covered areole appears in a slight depression in the apex of each tubercle. The areole bears as many as 6 dark brown or black, ⅛-of-an-inch-long spines. The flowers are often bell-shaped, about 1½ inches in diameter, 1 inch long, and bright yellow. The flowers grow from the apex.

origin
Chile

cultivation
The minimum temperature for the adult plant is 50°F (10°C). The plant needs partial shade from the direct rays of the sun and careful watering to avoid drowning the root. It is propagated through seeds.

flowering period
Late summer

Copiapoa laui

tribe
Cacteae

subtribe
Echinocactinae

description
Globular with a slightly flattened apex, dark olive-green, about ½–1 inch in diameter. There are as many as 20 slightly protruding, tuberculate ribs arranged spirally around the stem. A white felt-covered areole appears on the apex of each tubercle, with thin, white hairs and as many as 4 white spines growing from them. The apex is covered with the same white felt. The flowers grow from the apex, and they are open bell-shaped, about 1 inch in diameter, and yellow.

origin
Chile

cultivation
The minimum temperature for the adult plant is 50°F (10°C). The plant needs partial shading from the direct rays of the sun. It is propagated through seeds, but grafted specimens are most commonly available.

flowering period
Mid-summer

Coryphantha andreae

(NIPPLE CACTUS)

tribe
Cacteae

subtribe
Cactinae

description
Globular stem, may become slightly columnar with maturity, about 3½ inches in diameter and slightly taller. The curved apex is slightly concave with a white felt-covered centre. Tubercles encircle the stem, each protruding sharply, and measuring about 1 inch in diameter. A deep, felt-covered indentation extends from areoles along the upper edge of each tubercle. Radial spines, as many as 10 on a mature plant, measure about ½ an inch long and are curved toward the stem. These spines are yellow-grey with red-brown tips. There are 4–7 heavier central spines, the bottommost of which is as much as 1 inch in length and points straight down. The flowers have widely spreading petals of red and measure about 2½ inches in diameter.

origin
Mexico

cultivation
The minimum temperature for the adult plant is 50°F (10°C), although it can tolerate limited periods of lower temperatures. Exposure to sunlight should be limited during the summer months. It is propagated through seeds.

flowering period
Spring into summer

Coryphantha borwigii

tribe
Cacteae

subtribe
Cactinae

description
Globular, blue-green, about 2–4 inches in diameter, sometimes slightly columnar. Protruding tubercles are ¾ of an inch tall, 4-sided pyramidal-shaped. The areoles appear at the apices of the tubercles. They are covered with an off-white felt in younger plants but are naked in more mature specimens. Each areole has 8–10 heavy, radial spines and as many as 3 central spines. All the spines are about ¾ of an inch long and brown. The flowers are open bell-shaped, about 2½ inches in diameter, with 3 distinct rows of petals. The outermost row is burnt orange; the middle is yellow with burnt orange tips; and the innermost is yellow with a burnt orange line down the centre of each petal.

origin
Mexico

cultivation
The minimum temperature for the adult plant is 50°F (10°C). The plant needs direct sunlight, and is propagated through seeds.

flowering period
Summer

C

Coryphantha clavata
▲

tribe
Cacteae

subtribe
Cactinae

description
Columnar, curved at the apex, bluish-green, about 3 inches in diameter and as much as 8 inches in height. Additional stems may grow from the base when the inital stem reaches its mature height. The stem is covered in cone-shaped tubercles, about ¾ of an inch tall, with felt-encircled bases. A thin groove runs above each tubercle, holding a small red gland. Cream felt-covered areoles are located at the apex of each tubercle. With maturity, the areoles near the base of the stem drop from the plant, and are not replaced. Each areole has 6–10, red-brown radial spines, each about ½ an inch long. In addition, there is a longer, heavier yellowish central spine. The tubular flowers are about 2 inches long, brown with a central line of red on the outside and cream to yellow inside.

origin
Mexico

cultivation
The minimum temperature for the adult plant is 50°F (10°C), although it can tolerate brief periods at lower temperatures. However, full sunlight is needed. The plant is propagated through seeds.

flowering period
Spring into summer

Coryphantha elephantidens
▼

tribe
Cacteae

subtribe
Cactinae

description
Globular to flattened globular, with a rounded apex, dark olive-green, as much as 8 inches in diameter and 5½ inches tall. The surface is covered with tubercles, which are about 1½ inches tall and 2½ inches wide. The base of each tubercle is surrounded with white felt. Areoles appear in a depression at the tip of each tubercle. They have a minimal off-white felt covering and 6–8 inward-curving, yellowish, radial spines, each about ¾ of an inch long, with a dark brown tip. Flowers are open-petaled, about 4 inches in diameter, and orangish-red with some white on the inside and bright yellow stamens. They grow from the apex.

origin
Mexico

cultivation
The minimum temperature for the adult plant is 55°F (13°C). The plant needs direct sunlight, and is propagated through seeds or cuttings.

flowering period
Summer

Coryphantha erecta
▲

tribe
Cacteae

subtribe
Cactinae

description
Columnar with slight bending, eventually stooping to lie on the ground, curved at the apex with a cream felt-covered centre about 3 inches in diameter and as long as 12 inches, yellowish-green. It generally grows in colony-like clusters of stems shooting off from the base. Each stem is covered with cone-shaped ¼-inch tubercles that slant slightly upwards. Their bases are encircled with felt that partially hides a yellowish gland. Apical areoles are covered with a white felt on young plants. Each has 8–14, ½-an-inch long, yellow to brown, radial spines, which are horizontal to the stem. There are as many as 4 brown, 1-inch central spines, the bottommost of which is curved downward. Pale, burnt yellow flowers, each about 2–3 inches in diameter, grow across the apex of the stem.

origin
Mexico

cultivation
The minimum temperature for the adult plant is 50°F (10°C). The plant needs full sunlight throughout the year, but with a rest period during the winter. It is propagated through seeds.

flowering period
Spring into summer

Coryphantha palmeri

▼

tribe
Cacteae

subtribe
Cactinae

description
Globular, curved at apex, dark blue-green, about 3 inches in diameter. Cone-shaped tubercles, each about ¾ of an inch tall, are set in 13 spirals around the stem. An areole on the apex of each tubercle is covered in brownish-yellow felt on younger plants but completely bare in more mature plants. There are 10–14 heavy radial spines, which are golden with dark brown stripes. The single central spine grows at nearly a right angle to all of the radial spines. It is about ½ an inch long, brown and hooked at the tip. Its tubercles and areoles tend to become more dense in one part of the apex, creating a golden, felt-covered area. The flowers are tubular, pale yellow to cream, and about 1¼ inches long.

origin
Mexico

cultivation
The minimum temperature for the adult plant is 50°F (10°C). The plant needs moderate to full sunlight and a sandy, gravel-filled soil that is well drained. Watering should be done only when the soil feels very dry to the touch. It is propagated through seeds or shoots.

flowering period
Spring into summer

Discocactus horstii

▲

tribe
Cacteae

subtribe
Cactanae

description
Globular with a flattened and depressed apex, dark green, about 2½ inches in diameter and ¾ of an inch tall. There are as many as 20 protruding ribs, covered with comb-like areoles. The comb-like appearance is created by the 8–10 off-white, ⅛-of-an-inch-long spines. The centre of the apex is covered with off-white felt and ⅔-of-an-inch-long bristles. Its flowers are tubular, about 2½ inches in diameter, 3 inches long, and white in colour. They are nocturnal.

origin
Brazil

cultivation
The minimum temperature for the adult plant is 61°F (16°C). The plant needs direct sunlight and a soil that is rich in grit or sand. It is propagated through cuttings or seeds.

flowering period
Summer

E

Echinocactus grusonii
(GOLDEN BARREL CACTUS)

tribe
Cacteae

subtribe
Echinocactinae

description
Globular, concave at apex, dark green, about 3 feet in diameter and 3½ feet tall at maturity. The apex is covered with cream felt. There are 28–32 pronounced ribs, apically covered by the greenish-yellow felt of the areoles. Eight to 12 radial spines, each about 1 inch long, and 4 or 5 heavier central spines, each about 2 inches long, grow from the areole. All spines are bright yellow or golden throughout most of the plant's life, but become whitish in old age. The flowers are small tubes of brown hair-like petals, and yellow on the inside. They grow in a circle around the edge of the apex.

origin
Mexico

cultivation
The minimum temperature for the adult plant is 50°F (10°C). The plant tends to become discoloured when grown in a pot, unless it is protected from the direct rays of the sun during mid- to late summer. It is propagated through seeds.

flowering period
Summer

Echinocactus ingens
(LARGE BARREL CACTUS)

tribe
Cacteae

subtribe
Echinocactinae

description
Globular to cylindrical, slightly flattened at the apex, as much as 5 feet tall and 4 feet in diameter, yellowish-green. The centre of the apex is covered with yellowish felt. The surface is broken by 6–48 ribs, the number increasing with maturity. Elliptical areoles are covered with yellow felt. Each has 6–8 radial spines and 1 central spine. All spines are straight, thick, about 1 inch long, and grey with brown tips. The flowers are tubular, and about ¾ of an inch long.

origin
Mexico

cultivation
The minimum temperature for the adult plant is 59°F (15°C), although lower temperatures can be tolerated if the soil is dry. The plant needs full sunlight to encourage growth, which is very slow at best. It is propagated through seeds.

flowering period
Summer

Echinocereus adustus
(HEDGEHOG CACTUS)

tribe
Cacteae

subtribe
Echinocereinae

description
Flattened globular, green, about 3–4 inches in diameter and 1½–2½ inches tall. There are 12–15 ribs with close-set areoles, which are covered with light yellow felt and bear 16–20, thin, off-white, radial spines and 1, reddish-brown, ¾-of-an-inch-long, central spine. The radial spines intertwine with those of the areoles next to their own and cover nearly the entire surface of the plant. Its flowers are open-petaled, bell-shaped at the end of the tube, about 1½ inches in diameter and the same in length, with bright reddish-pink petals that have white edges. They appear near the apex.

origin
Mexico

cultivation
The minimum temperature for the adult plant is 50°F (10°C). The plant needs direct sunlight, and is propagated through seeds.

flowering period
Early summer

Echinocereus engelmannii
(STRAWBERRY CACTUS)

tribe
Cacteae

subtribe
Echinocereinae

description
Columnar with a rounded apex, pale brownish-green, about 2–3 inches in diameter and as much as 10 inches tall. The plant tends to send out shoots from its base, forming bunched colonies of similar specimens. There are 10–14 protruding ribs on each stem, with areoles set about ½ an inch apart. Each areole has 8–12, ½-an-inch-long, radial spines and as many as 6, 3-inch-long, central spines. The spines vary from off-white to grey to brown. The radial spines intertwine with those of the areoles next to their own. Its flowers are open, tubular, about 3 inches in diameter and in length, and are white or pink.

origin
Southwestern USA and Mexico

cultivation
The minimum temperature for the adult plant is 50°F (10°C). The plant needs direct sunlight, and is propagated through seeds or cuttings.

flowering period
Summer

E

Echinocereus enneacanthus

▲

tribe
Cacteae

subtribe
Echinocereinae

description
The curving, ribbed stems of this colony-growing plant resemble a group of pickles. It is columnar with definite curves, curved at the apex, yellowish-green to dark green, up to 8 inches long and 3 inches in diameter. The surface is broken by 6–10 tuberculate ribs, marked evenly at ¾ of an inch intervals with small areoles. Each areole has 8, yellowish, ½-an-inch-long, radial spines and 1, thicker, brown, central spine up to 2 inches in length. The plant sends out many branches from its base, creating a cluster of the species. The flowers are tubular, 2½ inches long and 3 inches in diameter, with red oblong petals. The fruit resembles a red raspberry about ¾ of an inch in diameter; it appears on the apex and has a strawberry-like taste.

origin
Southwestern USA, Mexico

cultivation
The minimum temperature for the adult plant is 50°F (10°C). It needs full sunlight, but also a winter rest period. The plant grows best in a well-drained sandy soil, and is propagated through cuttings.

flowering period
Summer

Echinocereus knippelianus

▼

tribe
Cacteae

subtribe
Echinocereinae

description
Globular to columnar with a slightly concave apex, dark green with yellowish or greyish splotches, about 4 inches tall and slightly less in diameter. The surface of the stem is broken by 5–7 protruding ribs. Each rib carries a few widely spaced, white, felt-covered areoles, and 1–3 short, bristle-like, curving, cream spines. On mature plants, the spines will have fallen from the areoles about the base. The plant grows from a tap-root into a cluster of stems. Its flowers are funnel-shaped, 1¼ inches long, and pink with widely opening petals. The flowers grow from areoles near the apex.

origin
Mexico

cultivation
The minimum temperature for the adult plant is 50°F (10°C), and it needs moderate to full sunlight. It is propagated through seeds.

flowering period
Summer

Echinocereus nivosus

▲

tribe
Cacteae

subtribe
Echinocereinae

description
Globular, pale green, about 1½ inches in diameter. The plant sends out many additional stems from its base, forming the clumped colony-like growths in which it is always found. Each stem has 10–12 slightly protruding ribs, with white felt-covered areoles spaced along them at ¼-of-an-inch intervals. Each areole has as many as 36, thin, ¼-of-an-inch-long, radial spines and 10–12, slightly heavier, ½–¾-of-an-inch-long, central spines. All spines are white with black tips. The radial spines intertwine with those of the areoles next to their own, hiding the entire surface of the plant. Flowers are open, bell-shaped, about 1¼ inches in diameter, and bright purplish-pink in colour. They grow near the apex.

origin
Mexico

cultivation
The minimum temperature for the adult plant is 50°F (10°C). The plant needs full sunlight and soil that has a slightly higher than normal limestone content. It is propagated through cuttings or seeds.

flowering period
Summer

Echinocereus pectinatus
(RAINBOW CACTUS)

tribe
Cacteae

subtribe
Echinocereinae

description
Columnar with a curved apex, blue-green, 6–8 inches long and about 2 inches in diameter. The surface is marked by as many as 20 ribs, which are wider at their bases. They are almost completely covered with protruding, round, cream and brown felt-covered areoles, which are much more closely set on the apex. From 20–25 white and pink radial spines grow from each areole. In addition, there are about 6 short, cream, central spines. The plant branches from the base, leading to a cluster of stems. Its flowers are funnel-shaped, opened very wide, about 3 inches in diameter, and with a spiny tube about 2½ inches long. Its petals are shimmering pink; stamens are yellow.

origin
Mexico

cultivation
The minimum temperature for the adult plant is 50°F (10°C). It needs full sunlight and a strict winter rest period, during which only the roots must be kept from drying out. Frequent water is needed during the summer. It is propagated through shoots or cuttings.

flowering period
Summer

Echinocereus pentalophus
(LADYFINGER OR HEDGEHOG CACTUS)

tribe
Cacteae

subtribe
Echinocereinae

description
Columnar but twisting and curving, laying on the ground for much of the stem's length of 5 inches, about ¾ of an inch in diameter, pale green. The plant sends out many stems from its base and grows in clusters. The surface of each stem is broken by 5 tuberculate ribs. These hold close-set, white areoles. As many as 6 radial spines, which are short and white with brown tips, grow from each areole. In addition, there may be a single darker central spine about ½ an inch long. The flowers are funnel-shaped, about 4 inches long with a hairy, spiny tube; the broad petals are pink-violet.

origin
Texas and Mexico

cultivation
The minimum temperature for the adult plant is 50°F (10°C). The plant needs full sunlight, and is propagated through cuttings.

flowering period
Summer

E

Echinocereus subinermis

tribe
Cacteae

subtribe
Echinocereinae

description
Columnar, with angular pointed apex, dark olive-green, about 3¼ inches thick and as much as 6 inches tall. The plant often grows in small groupings of stems growing from the same root. Each stem has 4–9 heavily protruding ribs, with distinct furrows between the ribs. In younger plants, grey felt-covered areoles have 3–10, ⅛-of-an-inch-long, off-white, radial spines and 1, ¼-of-an-inch-long, greyish, central spine. In more mature plants, the spines generally are missing. The flowers grow from a stem that appears near the apex. They are open-petaled, about 3¼ inches in diameter, and bright lemon-yellow.

origin
Mexico

cultivation
The minimum temperature for the adult plant is 50°F (10°C). The plant needs partial sunlight. It is propagated through cuttings or seeds.

flowering period
Summer

Echinocereus pulchellus

▲

tribe
Cacteae

subtribe
Echinocereinae

description
More or less globular plants, dark greyish-green, about 2 inches in diameter. The plant grows in small clumps, all emanating from a central, rock-like base. Each stem has 10–13 slightly protruding ribs. The white felt-covered areoles are located in notches along the stem. They have 2–4, cream-coloured, ½-an-inch-long, radial spines, but no central spines. Its flowers are open-petaled, growing at the end of tubes that spring from the sides of the stem, about 1½ inches in diameter, with petals that are bright purplish-pink with white edges and cream-yellow stamens.

origin
Mexico

cultivation
The minimum temperature for the adult plant is 50°F (10°C). The plant needs full sunlight, and is propagated through cuttings or seeds.

flowering period
Summer

Echinocereus trigiochidiatus
var. gonacanthus
(CLARET-CUP CACTUS)

tribe
Cacteae

subtribe
Echinocereinae

description
Globular with slightly flattened apex, olive-green, about 2½ inches in diameter. The plant tends to grow in small clusters of stems. Each stem has 6–10 heavily protruding ribs. The areoles are covered with greyish-white felt, and have 8, heavy, grey, ¾-of-an-inch-long, radial spines and 1, heavier, 2-inch-long, central spine that is yellow with a black tip. The flowers are open-petaled, about 2 inches in diameter, and bright orange with cream-yellow stamens. They grow on tubes that emerge from the sides of the stem.

origin
Southern USA

cultivation
The minimum temperature for the adult plant is 50°F (10°C). The plant needs full sunlight, and is propagated through cuttings or seeds.

flowering period
Summer

E

Echinocereus viridiflorus

var. davissi

tribe
Cacteae

subtribe
Echinocereinae

description
Depressed globular shape, very short, dull-green stems. The surface is broken by 6–7 ribs, and each areole has 9–12 radial spines (and occasionally 1 central spine), which are reddish or greyish, and up to ¾ of an inch long. Its flowers are funnel-shaped, about 1 inch long and ¾ of an inch wide, with greenish-yellow petals.

origin
Southwestern USA, Mexico

cultivation
The minimum temperature for the adult plant is 50°F (10°C). The plant needs moderate to full sunlight. It is propagated through seeds.

flowering period
Summer

Echinofossulocactus coptonogonus

var. cristata

tribe
Cacteae

subtribe
Echinocactinae

description
Globular, slightly concave at centre of an apex that is otherwise rounded, often wider than it is tall, olive-green, as much as 5 inches in diameter and up to 4 inches tall. In maturity, the stem will sprout additional shoots from its base. There are 10–14 pronounced ribs, separated by sharp edges, which often show a golden tan. Covered with cream-coloured felt, the areoles are about ¾ of an inch apart. There are 3–6 curving, ½-an-inch-long, red-brown to grey radial spines growing from each areole,

and 1 central spine that is similar but as much as ½ an inch longer. The flowers are about 1 inch long, with grey-white outside petals and white-edged reddish inside petals. They grow around the apex. The crested form of the species (shown here) is only discovered on rare occasions; a careful examination of its spination will reveal which kind it is.

origin
Mexico

cultivation
The minimum temperature for the adult plant is 50°F (10°C). The plant needs shelter from the direct rays of the sun during the hottest part of the summer day. It is propagated through seeds or shoots.

flowering period
Spring

Echinofossulocactus erectocentrus

tribe
Cacteae

subtribe
Echinocactinae

description
Globular with a flattened apex, greyish-green, about 3½ inches in diameter and 2 inches tall. There are as many as 50–60 ribs, with yellowish felt-covered areoles spaced about ½ an inch apart. Each areole has 4–6, pale tan, radial spines which are ½ an inch long, although one of them is as long as 2 inches. Overall, the plant looks like a clump of drying grass. Its flowers are tubular, about ¾ of an inch long, and greyish-white in colour.

origin
Mexico

cultivation
The minimum temperature for the adult plant is 50°F (10°C). The plant needs partial sunlight, and is propagated through seeds.

flowering period
Summer

E

Echinofossulocactus multicostatus

▼

tribe
Cacteae

subtribe
Echinocactinae

description
Globular with a flattened apex, dark green, about 4 inches in diameter. There are as many as 100 ribs, each bearing just 1–3 white felt-covered areoles. The areoles have 6–10, 1–1½-inch-long, yellow to grey spines that intertwine with the spines of the areoles next to their own and cover the entire surface of the plant. The flowers are open, tubular, about 1 inch in diameter and the same in length, with pinkish petals with central lines of purple and yellow stamens.

origin
Mexico

cultivation
The minimum temperature for the adult plant is 45°F (10°C). The plant needs full sunlight, and is propagated through seeds.

flowering period
Late spring

Echinomastus durangensis

▲

tribe
Cacteae

subtribe
Echinocactinae

description
Slightly columnar with a rounded apex, dark green, about 2–3 inches in diameter and about 3–4 inches tall. The plant grows as a single stem. There are 18 ribs, further divided horizontally into ¼-of-an-inch-tall tubercles. An areole, heavily covered with white felt, appears at the apex of each tubercle, with as many as three dozen, ½–1-inch-long, grey, radial spines and 4 similar central spines that all point upward. The radial spines intertwine with those of the areoles next to their own, covering the surface of the plant. The flowers are open-petaled, about ¾–1 inch in diameter, and are brownish-red with cream-yellow stamens.

origin
Mexico

cultivation
The minimum temperature for the adult plant is 50°F (10°C). The plant needs full sunlight. It is propagated through seeds.

flowering period
Summer

E

Echinomastus intertextus

tribe
Cacteae

subtribe
Echinocactinae

description
Globular to very slightly columnar, dark green, about 3 inches in diameter and as much as 4 inches tall. There are 12–14 tuberculate ribs with scattered areoles. Each areole has 16–24, ½-an-inch-long, reddish, radial spines and 4, ¾-of-an-inch-long, reddish, central spines. The spines curve inward and intertwine with those of the areoles next to their own, giving the plant an appearance something like that of a ball of yarn. The flowers are open-petaled, about ¾ of an inch in diameter, pinkish-white with pale yellow stamens and a red stigma. They grow from the apex.

origin
Southwestern USA

cultivation
The minimum temperature for the adult plant is 50°F (10°C). The plant needs full sunlight and a soil that has a slightly elevated content of limestone. It is propagated through seeds.

flowering period
Summer

Echinomastus unguispinus

tribe
Cacteae

subtribe
Echinocactinae

description
Globular with a slightly flattened apex, dark blue-green, about 4 inches in diameter and as much as 5 inches tall. There are no ribs, but scattered, white felt-coverd areoles. Each areole has as many as 2 dozen, ¾-of-an-inch-long, blue-white, radial spines and as many as 8, heavier, slightly longer, reddish-brown, central spines. The radial spines intertwine with those of the areoles next to their own, covering the entire surface of the plant. Its flowers are open bell-shaped, about 1 inch in diameter and in length, and are reddish-brown with yellow stamens. They grow from the centre of the apex.

origin
Mexico

cultivation
The minimum temperature for the adult plant is 50°F (10°C). The plant needs full sunlight, as well as a soil that is well-drained, and slightly high in limestone and grit. It is propagated through seeds.

flowering period
Summer

Echinopsis aurea
▲

tribe
Cacteae

subtribe
Echinocereinae

description
Globular to columnar, with a rounded apex, dark green, as much as 2½ inches in diameter and as tall as 4 inches. Each stem tends to produce many offshoots at its base, forming substantial colonies. There are 12–14 sharp-edged ribs, further separated by horizontal notches. Areoles on young plants are coverd by tan felt. They are naked on mature plants. Ten to 12, thin, white, radial spines, measuring about ½-an-inch-long, and as many as 4, heavier, brownish, central spines grow from each areole. Flowers are about 4 inches in diameter, with petals that are burnt orange on the outside, bright yellow on the inside, and have a green-white tube. The stamens are cream-coloured. The flowers grow from the sides of the stem.

origin
Argentina

cultivation
The minimum temperature for the adult plant is 50°F (10°C). The plant needs full sunlight and well-drained soil. It is propagated through shoots or cuttings.

flowering period
Spring

Echinopsis aurea
var. aurantiaca
▼

tribe
Cacteae

subtribe
Echinocereinae

description
Globular, dark olive-green, about 3–4 inches in diameter. There are as many as 16 ribs with large, yellowish felt-covered areoles. Each areole has 6–10, ¼-of-an-inch-long, tan, radial spines and as many as 4, slightly longer, brown, central spines. Flowers are open, bell-petaled, about 2½ inches long, and bright reddish-orange with yellow stamens. They grow from near the apex.

origin
Argentina

cultivation
The minimum temperature for the adult plant is 50°F (10°C). The plant needs full sunlight. It is propagated through seeds.

flowering period
Summer

E

Echinopsis "Haku-jo"

▲

tribe
Cacteae

subtribe
Echinocereinae

description
Columnar, dark olive-green, about
3 inches in diameter and as much as
6 inches tall. The plant produces many
smaller versions of itself, both from its
base and along one of its sides. There are
as many as 16 ribs on each stem, some
entirely covered with off-white felt and
others covered only at the areoles.
Each areole has as many as 8, yellowish-
brown, ¼-of-an-inch-long, radial spines
and 1 or 2, ½-an-inch-long, brown,
central spines. Flowers are tubular,
about 3 inches in diameter and 4 inches
long, and white in colour. The exact
origins of this plant have not been
confirmed and there are those who
believe it to be a mutation.

origin
Japan

cultivation
The minimum temperature for the adult
plant is 55°F (13°C). The plant needs
partial shade, and is propagated through
cuttings.

flowering period
Summer

Echinopsis kermesina
(EASTER LILY CACTUS)

▼

tribe
Cacteae

subtribe
Echinocereinae

description
Globular with completely rounded apex,
blue-green, about 6–8 inches in diameter
at maturity. There are 14–24 ribs,
further divided horizontally by grooves,
where the white felt-covered areoles
occur. It has 10–16 thin, ½-an-inch-
long, yellow, radial spines, most with
brownish tips, and about 6, 1-inch-long,
slightly curved, central spines. The plant
generally grows in small colonies.
Its flowers are tubular, about 6 inches
long and 3½ inches in diameter, with
reddish petals and white felt-covered
areoles along the tube. They grow
near the apex.

origin
Argentina

cultivation
The minimum temperature for the adult
plant is 55°F (13°C). The plant needs
full sunlight and regular, but not too
heavy, watering through the summer.
It is propagated through seeds.

flowering period
Spring

E

x Epicactus "Augusta von Szombathy"
(ORCHID CACTUS)

▲

tribe
Cacteae

subtribe
intergeneric hybrid

description
Hanging or prostrate, angular, green
stems growing from a central root, each
as much as 2½ feet long and about
1¼ inches at their widest diameter.
There are as many as 8 heavily
protruding ribs, but no spines.
The flowers are a variety of colours
and shades, open funnel-shaped,
about 3–4 inches in diameter and
4–4½ inches long. The plant is a long-
standing hybrid, developed in the 1930s
by Curt Knebel of Germany.

origin
Germany

cultivation
The minimum temperature for the adult
plant is 50°F (10°C). The plant needs
shade from the direct rays of the sun, and
is propagated through cuttings.

flowering period
Late spring

x Epicactus "Deutsche Kaiserin"
(ORCHID CACTUS)

▼

tribe
Cacteae

subtribe
intergeneric hybrid

description
Green, leaf-like pads grow at the ends of
heavy, hanging then upward-curving
green stems, and produce additional,
thinner pads from their undulating
edges. There are scattered, thorn-like
areoles. The flowers are funnel-shaped,
and bright pink with whitish interiors.
They grow in considerable numbers from
the edges of both the leaf-like pads and
the thinner pads that grow from them.
This is a domestically produced hybrid of
the species *Nopalxochia phyllanthoides*,
which was developed in Germany.

origin
Germany

cultivation
The minimum temperature for the adult
plant is 55°F (13°C). The plant needs
shade from the direct rays of the sun, and
is propagated through cuttings.

flowering period
Mid-spring through mid-summer

E

x Epicactus "Sweet Alibi"
(ORCHID CACTUS)

▲

tribe
Cacteae

subtribe
intergeneric hybrid

description
Erect leaf-like pads growing from a
central root, grey-green. The serrated
edges of the pads carry spineless,
greyish felt-covered areoles. Its flowers
grow from some of these areoles, and
they are open funnel-shaped, as much as
6 inches in diameter, with pale pink
petals and cream stamens. The plant is a
hybrid produced in the USA.

origin
USA

cultivation
The minimum temperature for the adult
plant is 50°F (10°C). The plant needs
protection from the direct rays of the
sun. It is propagated through cuttings.

flowering period
Spring

x Epicactus "Sky Rocket"
(ORCHID CACTUS)

▲

tribe
Cacteae

subtribe
intergeneric hybrid

description
Green, leaf-like pads grow at the ends of
heavy, hanging then upward-curving,
green stems, and produce additional,
thinner pads from their undulating
edges. Flowers are open funnel-shaped,
about 6 inches in diameter, bright
reddish-orange with a dark red style.
They are produced at the ends of long
stems that grow from the pads. This is a
domestically produced hybrid of long
standing, developing in the 1930s
in the USA.

origin
USA

cultivation
The minimum temperature for the adult
plant is 50°F (10°C). The plant needs
shade from the direct rays of the sun, and
is propagated through cuttings.

flowering period
Spring

Epithelantha micromeris
(BUTTON CACTUS)

tribe
Cacteae

subtribe
Echinocactinae

description
Globular to slightly columnar, with a rounded but slightly concave apex, about 1–2½ inches in diameter and as tall as 3 inches. The stem is green, but that colour is difficult to see through the heavy, tightly woven white spines that tend to cover the entire surface. Most of the spines are no more than ⅛ of an inch in length, although new areoles often do sport longer spines which soon break off. Flowers are long, pipe-like structures with a rounded apex, and are light pink with a white dot at the apex. They grow straight up in clusters from the centre of the apex. The plant also produces red berries at the base of the flowers. It is common to find this plant as colonies of shoots growing from the base of a main stem.

origin
Texas and Mexico

cultivation
The minimum temperature for the adult plant is 50°F (10°C). The plant grows best in a soil with a high concentration of limestone — as much as 25 per cent by content. It is propagated through seeds.

flowering period
Summer

Epithelantha micromeris
var. bokei

tribe
Cacteae

subtribe
Echinocactinae

description
Globular, green, about 2 inches in diameter. The surface of the stem is covered with tiny tubercles, each with a white felt-covered areole. Varying but large numbers of thin, inward-curving, white, radial spines grow from each areole, intertwining tightly with those of the areoles next to their own and covering the entire surface of the plant. The overall appearance of the plant, from directly above, is very much that of a golfball. Its flowers are open bell-shaped, about ½ an inch in diameter, and silvery pink with cream-yellow stamens. They appear at the centre of the apex.

origin
Texas and Mexico

cultivation
The minimum temperature for the adult plant is 50°F (10°C). The plant requires full sunlight and constantly warm temperatures, and is propagated through seeds or cuttings.

flowering period
Summer

E

Epithelantha micromeris

var. greggii

tribe
Cacteae

subtribe
Echinocactinae

description
Globular to columnar with a rounded apex, dark green, about 2 inches in diameter and as much as 3½ inches tall. Tubercles cover the surface of the plant, each with a white felt-covered areole. The areoles have a varying but large number of ¼-of-an-inch-long, white to yellowish, radial spines and as many as 3, slightly longer, central spines. The radial spines intertwine with those of the areoles next to their own, covering the entire surface of the plant. Flowers are tubular, about ½ an inch in diameter, and pink. They grow from the centre of the apex.

origin
Mexico

cultivation
The minimum temperature for the adult plant is 50°F (10°C). The plant requires full sunlight and constantly warm temperatures. It is propagated through seeds or cuttings.

flowering period
Summer

Epithelantha micromeris

var. unguispina

▼ ▼

tribe
Cacteae

subtribe
Echinocactinae

description
Globular to columnar with a rounded apex, dark green, about 2 inches in diameter and as much as 3½ inches tall. Tubercles cover the surface of the plant, each with a bright snow-white felt-covered areole. These have a varying but large number of ¼–½-an-inch-long, hair-like, radial spines and 1, longer, central spine. The radial spines intertwine with those of the areoles next to their own, covering the entire surface of the plant, but not nearly as densely as others of this species. The centre of the apex is covered with bright snow-white felt. Its flowers are open funnel-shaped, about ½ an inch in diameter, and glossy pink. They grow from the centre of the apex.

origin
Mexico

cultivation
The minimum temperature for the adult plant is 50°F (10°C). The plant requires full sunlight and constantly warm temperatures. It is propagated through seeds or cuttings.

flowering period
Summer

Eriocereus jusbertii

tribe
Cacteae

subtribe
Cereinae

description
Elongated, angular stems, green, about
1½–2 inches in diameter and varying in
length. There are 4–6 protruding ribs
with yellow felt-covered areoles spaced
at about ¾-of-an-inch intervals. Each
areole has as many as 8, dark brown,
¼-of-an-inch-long, radial spines and as
many as 4, slightly longer, black central
spines. The flowers are open-petaled, as
much as 8 inches in diameter, with thin
cream-white petals and stamens. Some of
the outer petals have a brownish tint.
The flowers grow from the sides of
the stems and are nocturnal.

origin
Argentina

cultivation
The minimum temperature for the adult
plant is 50°F (10°C). The plant needs
partial shade from the direct rays of
the sun. It is propagated through
cuttings or seeds.

flowering period
Mid-summer

Escobaria chaffeyi

tribe
Cacteae

subtribe
Cactinae

description
Columnar with a rounded apex, dark
olive-green, about 2–3 inches in
diameter and as much as 5 inches tall.
The surface is covered with tubercles,
each with a white felt-covered aerole.
As many as 20, white, ¼-of-an-inch-
long, bristly, radial spines and up to 3,
brown-tipped, slightly shorter, central
spines grow from each areole. Flowers
are open bell-shaped, about ½ an inch in
diameter and ¾ of an inch long, with
petals that are brownish-pink with
cream-coloured edges. They grow
from the centre of the apex.

origin
Mexico

cultivation
The minimum temperature for the adult
plant is 50°F (10°C). The plant
needs full sunlight. It is propagated
through seeds.

flowering period
Summer

E

Espostoa lanata
(OLD-LADY CACTUS)

◄

tribe
Cacteae

subtribe
Cereinae

description
Columnar with a near tree-like canopy of stems branching from the upper reaches of the trunk, which can grow as tall as 12–14 feet. The branches are 1½–4 inches in diameter, and rounded at the apex. The surface of the plant is dark green, but it is mostly masked on the younger areas with white hairs growing from the areoles. These silky hairs are noticeably thicker on the apex of each stem. There are 18–28 rounded ribs, with areoles about ¼ of an inch apart, which alternate with those on the ribs to either side. Each areole has 1 or 2 heavy, brownish, central spines, each as long as 3 inches, that point directly outward. Its flowers are white, 2-inch-long tubes that open only at night. They grow just below the apex.

origin
Peru

cultivation
The minimum temperature for the adult plant is 50°F (10°C). The plant will do well in partially shaded or full-sun locations, so long as it is provided with constant heat through the winter. It is propagated through cuttings.

flowering period
Summer

Espostoa nana

▲

tribe
Cacteae

subtribe
Cereinae

description
Columnar with a rounded apex, about
3–3½ inches in diameter and as much as
5 feet in height. The plant generally
produces additional branching stems
from its base. There are as many as 30
protruding ribs on a mature stem. Each
carries grey felt-covered areoles set at an
interval of about ¼ of an inch. The
areoles have as many as 32, grey, ¼-of-
an-inch-long, radial spines and 1, slightly
longer, central spine. The entire surface
of the plant is covered with a white wool,
which appears to have been spun about
the stem. This wool forms into
something like a cotton ball on top of the
apex. The flowers are tubular, about
1½–2 inches long, and white in colour.
They are nocturnal and grow from
the apex.

origin
Peru

cultivation
The minimum temperature for the adult
plant is 55°F (13°C). The plant needs
full sunlight and great care should be
taken to avoid over-watering. It is
propagated through cuttings or seeds.

flowering period
Summer

Espostoa ritteri

▼

tribe
Cacteae

subtribe
Cereinae

description
Columnar main stem, as tall as 13 feet,
that branches into a near tree-like
canopy of 2¾-inch diameter branches,
dark green. There are about 20 ribs, each
broken by transverse depressions. The
areoles are located between these
depressions. They are covered with
white felt and sport white hairs of
¾–1¼ inches in length. There are about
2 dozen thin, short, grey, radial spines of
about ¼ of an inch in length and 1
longer, white, central spine of as much as
¾ of an inch in length. A long cephalium,
covered with yellow to orange hair,
extends along the upper side of the stem.
It is here that the 3-inch-long, tubular,
white flowers grow, as well as round,
red, scaly fruit.

origin
Peru

cultivation
The minimum temperature for the adult
plant is 55°F (13°C). Specimens under
cultivation rarely produce flowers. The
plant is propagated through seeds.

flowering period
Summer

Ferocactus acanthodes
(DESERT BARREL CACTUS)

tribe
Cacteae

subtribe
Echinocactinae

description
This plant begins life as a small, blue-green, globular plant. In maturity, it is a dark green, columnar plant of as much as 10 feet in height. Also, in maturity, there are as many as 26 ribs, carrying the close-set, yellow felt-covered areoles. There are about a dozen, 1½-inch-long, radial spines, striped or splotched with white and various shades of red. In addition, there are 4 central spines, which are about 4 inches long and curved. The flowers are tubular, about 1½–2 inches long and 2–3 inches in diameter, purple and scaly along the tube and yellow or orange in the petals.

origin
Southwestern USA

cultivation
The minimum temperature for the adult plant is 50°F (10°C). Plants under cultivation tend not to grow nearly as tall as those in the wild. They need full sunlight and continuous mild heat throughout the winter, and do best with a soil that is rich, but well-drained. The plant is propagated through seeds.

flowering period
Summer

Ferocactus emoryi
(COVILLE BARREL CACTUS)

tribe
Cacteae

subtribe
Echinocactinae

description
Spherical when younger, becoming columnar with a rounded apex as it ages, this species has a maximum diameter of 1 foot and a height of 7 feet. The stem has between 20–30 noticeably protruding ribs, each with 6–8 curved, radial spines, 2 inches long, and 1 slightly longer straight central spine which is hooked at its end. All spines vary in colour from white to shades of red. The tubular flowers are red, about 2½ inches long and 2 inches in diameter, appearing around the apex.

origin
Southwestern USA and northern Mexico

cultivation
The minimum temperature for the adult plant is 50°F (10°C). The plant needs full sunlight. It is propagated through seeds.

flowering period
Late spring through summer

Ferocactus gracilis

tribe
Cacteae

subtribe
Echinocactinae

description
Columnar with a rounded apex, dark olive-green, about 10 inches–1 foot in diameter and as tall as 10 feet. There are 12–24, protruding, cone-shaped ribs, bearing white felt-covered areoles. Five, thin, white, radial spines, about 1½ inches long, and 6–14, red, layered, central spines, grow from each aerole. One of the central spines is flattened top and bottom, and much wider than the others. The flowers are about 1½ inches long with petals that are yellow with a red line down their centre. The fruit is yellow and round.

origin
Mexico

cultivation
The minimum temperature for the adult plant is 50°F (10°C). The plant needs full sunlight, and does best with a soil that carries a good proportion of mineral salts. It is propagated through seeds.

flowering period
Spring into summer

Ferocactus haematacanthus

tribe
Cacteae

subtribe
Echinocactinae

description
Globular to columnar, bright lime-green, as much as 1½ feet in diameter and 3 feet 4 inches tall. There are 12–30 heavily protruding ribs with grey felt-covered areoles spaced at 1½-inch intervals. Each aerole has 6, white-tipped red, radial spines and 2, white, central spines, all of which range from ¾–1½ inches in length. Its flowers are open funnel-shaped, about 3 inches in diameter, the same in length, and deep red in colour. They grow from the apex, which has a central area of yellow and red bristles.

origin
Mexico

cultivation
The minimum temperature for the adult plant is 50°F (10°C). The plant needs full sunlight and a soil with a slightly elevated lime content. It is propagated through seeds.

flowering period
Summer

Ferocactus hamatacanthus

(TURK'S HEAD)

tribe
Cacteae

subtribe
Echinocactinae

description
Globular to slightly columnar, with a rounded apex, blue-green, as much as 1½ feet in diameter and 2 feet tall. There are about a dozen pronounced ribs, further separated by transverse depressions. The large, white felt-covered areoles occur between the depressions at intervals of about 1¼ inches. Nectar glands of less than ⅙ of an inch in length can often be seen in the areoles at the apex that produce the flowers. Eight to 12, ½–2-inch-long, reddish, radial spines and as many as 4 straight, white, central spines with hooked ends grow from the areoles. The flowers are tubular, about 3 inches long, with yellow petals that are reddish on the inside. They grow from the centre of the apex. The fruit is purplish-brown, with a few large white scales, and measures about 1–2 inches long.

origin
Texas and Mexico

cultivation
The minimum temperature for the adult plant is 45°F (7°C). The plant needs protection from cold temperatures. It is propagated through seeds.

flowering period
Spring into summer

F

Ferocactus herrerae

tribe
Cacteae

subtribe
Echinocactinae

description
Globular to columnar with a rounded apex, dark green, as much as 1½ feet in diameter and 6 feet tall. There are 12–14 heavily protruding, wavy ribs with long, white felt-covered areoles extending along their lengths. Each areole has 8–10, ½-an-inch-long, off-white, radial spines and 1, 1-inch-long, central spine with a hooked tip. Flowers are open funnel-shaped, about 3 inches in diameter and in length, with petals that are red with yellow edges. They grow near the apex.

origin
Mexico

cultivation
The minimum temperature for the adult plant is 50°F (10°C). The plant needs full sunlight, and is propagated through seeds.

flowering period
Summer

Ferocactus latispinus

tribe
Cacteae

subtribe
Echinocactinae

description
Globular, sometimes columnar, bright lime-green, as much as 1 foot 4 inches in diameter. There are 8–20 ribs, further divided by notches that give the ribs a layered effect from top to bottom. The areoles are covered with white felt and located about 1½ inches apart. There are 6–12, thin, white, radial spines, about 1 inch in length, and 4–6, thicker, longer, red to yellow, central spines. The bottommost of each areole's central spines is flattened, curves downward and has a hook at the tip. Flowers are tubular, about 1½ inches long, with white to various shades of red petals. The fruit is about 1½ inches long and reddish.

origin
Mexico

cultivation
The minimum temperature for the adult plant is 50°F (10°C). The plant is propagated through seeds.

flowering period
Spring into summer

71

F

Ferocactus pottsii

▲

tribe
Cacteae

subtribe
Echinocactinae

description
Globular, dull olive-green, about 1 foot
in diameter. There are 8–16 heavily
protruding ribs with white felt-covered,
oblong radials spaced at intervals of
about 1 inch. Each areole has 8–10,
grey, ½–¾-of-an-inch-long, radial
spines and as many as 4, reddish, 1–1½-
inch-long, central spines. The flowers
are open funnel-shaped, about 1½–2½
inches in diameter and the same in length.
They are yellow with some brownish-red
at the base of the outside petals. They
grow near the off-white felt-covered
centre of the slightly flattened apex.

origin
Mexico

cultivation
The minimum temperature for the adult
plant is 45°F (7°C). The plant needs
full sunlight, and is propagated
through seeds.

flowering period
Mid-summer

Ferocactus robustus

▼

tribe
Cacteae

subtribe
Echinocactinae

description
Globular, bright lime-green, about
8 inches in diameter. The plant branches
profusely at the base, producing a colony
that can be as much as 10 feet in
diameter. Each stem has 8–10 ribs, with
sporadically notched edges. Areoles,
which alternate with those on either side
of them, are covered with brown to grey
felt. There about 12–14, grey, radial
spines, each about 1½–2 inches long,
and as many as 6, heavier, reddish,
central spines, measuring as long as
2½ inches. The flowers are tubular,
about 1½ inches long, with yellow petals
and a scaly tube. The fruit is round,
about 1 inch in diameter, red and scaly.

origin
Mexico

cultivation
The minimum temperature for the adult
plant is 50°F (10°C). Under cultivation
the plant generally will not create as
large a colony as it would in the wild,
however it does spread profusely. It is
propagated through shoots or seeds.

flowering period
Spring into summer

F

Ferocactus wislizenii
var. tiburonensis
(FISHHOOK BARREL CACTUS)

tribe
Cacteae

subtribe
Echinocactinae

description
Globular (in youth) to columnar with a rounded apex (in maturity), green with some yellowish tinting, as tall as 6½ feet. There are as many as 2 dozen, sharply protruding ribs, serrated between the large areoles, which are covered with grey to brown felt and slightly depressed into the rib. Young plants do not carry any radial spines, but in mature plants these are about 2 inches long and grey-white in colour, and may number as many as 10. The 6–9 central spines are heavier, and greyish-red. One of the central spines is much thicker and as much as 6 inches in length. There is a heavy hook at the end of this spine. The flowers are bell-shaped, about 2½ inches long, with green outer petals and yellow to red inner petals. The fruit is about 2 inches long and yellowish.

origin
Southwestern USA and Mexico

cultivation
The minimum temperature for the adult plant is 45°F (7°C). The plant needs full light through as much of the year as possible. It is propagated through seeds.

flowering period
Summer

Frailea asteroides

tribe
Cacteae

subtribe
Echinocactinae

description
Globular, greyish-brown, about 1 inch in diameter. There are 10–14 slightly protruding ribs, separated by heavy indentations, each with a bead-like row of close-set, grey felt-covered areoles. Each areole has 8, miniscule, brown, radial spines. The flowers are open bell-shaped, about 1½ inches in diameter, and creamy yellow. They appear in great profusion from the centre of the slightly concave apex and offer an overall bloom area much larger than the plant itself.

origin
Brazil

cultivation
The minimum temperature for the adult plant is 55°F (13°C). The plant needs full sunlight, particularly during the flowering period, and a well-drained, slightly acidic soil. It is propagated through seeds.

flowering period
Summer

Frailea curvispina

G

Frailea curvispina

tribe
Cacteae

subtribe
Echinocactinae

description
Columnar with a rounded, slightly concave apex, dark green, about 1 inch in diameter and 2 inches tall. There are 3 dozen or more ribs with very pimply surfaces and yellow felt-covered aeroles. Each areole has as many as 16, yellowish, downward-curving, ¼-of-an-inch-long, radial spines and one, slightly longer, central spine. Mature plants produce smaller replicas of themselves from the edges of the apex. Flowers are open-petaled, about 1 inch in diameter, and pale yellow. They appear near the apex.

origin
Brazil

cultivation
The minimum temperature for the adult plant is 55°F (13°C). The plant needs full sunlight and constantly warm temperatures, as well as a well-drained, slightly acidic soil. It is propagated through cuttings or seeds.

flowering period
Summer

Gymnocactus gielsdorfiana

tribe
Cacteae

subtribe
Echinocactinae

description
Globular to slightly columnar with a rounded apex, yellowish-green, about 2 inches in diameter and as much as 3 inches tall. The surface of the stem is tuberculate, arranged spirally around the plant. Areoles are pyramid-shaped and appear at the apex of each tubercle. They are covered in white felt. They have 6–8, ¾-of-an-inch-long, black-tipped white, radial spines. The axils are bare. Flowers are open-petaled, about 1 inch long, white and with a creamy tint at the centre. They appear near the apex.

origin
Mexico

cultivation
The minimum temperature for the adult plant is 50°F (10°C). It needs full sunlight and a well-drained, mineral-enriched soil. The plant is propagated through seeds.

flowering period
Summer

Gymnocactus subterraneus

var. zaragosae

tribe
Cacteae

subtribe
Echinocactinae

description
Club-like, about 2–3 inches long and 1–1½ inches in diameter tapering to a much thinner base, green. The tuberculate surface is covered with grey-white felt-covered areoles that become almost hairy at flowering time. Each areole has as many as 2 dozen, ¼-of-an-inch-long, brown-tipped white, radial spines and two ½-an-inch-long, black, central spines. The flowers are funnel-shaped, about ½ an inch in diameter, ¾ of an inch in length, and orangish-yellow in colour. They appear from the apex. The plant is often found growing on almost vertical surfaces – a feat made possible by its extremely long tap-root. It is also generally found in small groupings.

origin
Mexico

cultivation
The minimum temperature for the adult plant is 50°F (10°C). It needs full sunlight and a soil with a slightly elevated content of lime. The plant is propagated through cuttings or seeds.

flowering period
Summer

Gymnocalycium cardenasianum
(CHIN CACTUS)

tribe
Cacteae

subtribe
Echinocactinae

description
Globular with a slightly concave apex, pale blue-green, from 4–10 inches in diameter. There are 8–10, protruding but rounded ribs separated by strong indentations. They have white, felt-covered areoles with as many as 6, grey-white, curving, 2½-inch-long, radial spines and 1 or 2, similar but longer, central spines. The flowers are open-petaled funnel-shaped, about 3½ inches in diameter, 2½ inches tall, and pinkish in colour. They grow near the apex.

origin
Bolivia

cultivation
The minimum temperature for the adult plant is 50°F (10°C). The plant needs partial shade, and is propagated through seeds.

flowering period
Early summer

Gymnocactus viereckii

tribe
Cacteae

subtribe
Echinocactinae

description
Oblong, blue-green, about 1¾ inches in diameter and 1 inch tall. There are 12–18 tuberculate ribs with white felt-covered areoles. Each areole has as many as 20, white, ½-an-inch-long, radial spines and as many as 4, black, ¾-of-an-inch-long, central spines. The radial spines intertwine with those of the areoles next to their own, covering the entire surface of the stem. Flowers are open bell-shaped, about ¾-of-an-inch in diameter and in length, and have purplish-pink petals with cream-yellow stamens. They grow from the centre of the apex.

origin
Mexico

cultivation
The minimum temperature for the adult plant is 50°F (10°C), and it needs indirect sunlight and a soil that has a slightly elevated lime content. The plant is propagated through seeds.

flowering period
Summer

G

Gymnocalycium denudatum
(SPIDER CACTUS)

▲

tribe
Cacteae

subtribe
Echinocactinae

description
Globular with a concave centre to its apex, dark grey-green, from 3–6 inches in diameter. There are 6–8 large, protruding, rounded, ribs separated by deep indentations. They each have only 2 sets of 3, widely spaced, grey felt-covered areoles, with 4–8, ¾-of-an-inch-long, radial spines that are prostrate on the surface of the stem. The flowers are open-petaled bell-shaped, about 3 inches in diameter and 2 inches long, with white petals with cream stamens. They grow from the apex.

origin
Argentina

cultivation
The minimum temperature for the adult plant is 50°F (10°C). It needs partial shade, and is propagated through seeds.

flowering period
Mid-summer

Gymnocalycium mihanovichii
(PLAID CACTUS)

tribe
Cacteae

subtribe
Echinocactinae

description
Globular, reddish-green, about 2½ inches in diameter. There are as many as 8, heavily protruding, side-veined ribs with areoles that are covered with a ball of white felt. Each areole has 4–6, brownish, ½-an-inch-long, radial spines. Flowers are open-petaled, about 2 inches in diameter, and bright pink. They grow at the end of a long tube that sprouts from near the apex.

origin
Paraguay

cultivation
The minimum temperature for the adult plant is 50°F (10°C), and it needs partial shade. The plant is propagated through seeds.

flowering period
Early summer

Gymnocalycium quehlianum
(DWARF CHIN CACTUS)

▲

tribe
Cacteae

subtribe
Echinocactinae

description
Globular, greyish-green, as much as 3 inches in diameter. There are as many as 12 protruding ribs, further divided horizontally into tubercle-like segments. Each segment has one grey felt-covered areole with 2–5, yellowish, heavily curved, ½-an-inch-long, radial spines. The flowers are funnel-shaped, about 2–3 inches long, and white with a reddish tube.

origin
Argentina

cultivation
The minimum temperature for the adult plant is 50°F (10°C). It needs bright sunlight, and is propagated through seeds or cuttings.

flowering period
Mid-summer

Gymnocalycium saglionis
(GIANT CHIN CACTUS)

▼

tribe
Cacteae

subtribe
Echinocactinae

description
Globular, bright green, as much as 1 foot in diameter. There are 10–12 undulating ribs, with rounded tubercles. One grey felt-covered areole grows at the apex of each tubercle, with 7–15, grey to brown, 2-inch-long, radial spines and as many as 3, black, 1½-inch-long, central spines. The flowers are open-petaled bell-shaped, about 1¼ inches long, and pale pink with yellow stamens. The plants grow in small groupings.

origin
Argentina

cultivation
The minimum temperature for the adult plant is 50°F (10°C), and it needs partial shade. The plant is propagated through cuttings or seeds.

flowering period
Mid-summer

Homalocephala texensis
(HORSE CRIPPLER OR DEVIL'S HEAD OR CANDY CACTUS)

▲

tribe
Cacteae

subtribe
Echinocactinae

description
Globular, slightly flattened at the apex, blue-green, about 1 foot in diameter and 6 inches tall. The apex has an irregularly shaped central area that is covered with cream felt. The surface of the stem is broken by 12–26 pronounced ribs, each with 2–7 large, cream felt-covered areoles. Each areole has 5–7, thick, worm-like, radial spines, which are about 1 inch long. They are pink in younger plants, but take on a yellowish tint in more mature plants. A single central spine is similar but as much as 2½ inches in length. The flowers are tubular (with scales), about 2½ inches wide and deep, and are various shades of red fading from darker to lighter toward the centre; outer petals have a spiny tip. The fruit is round and red.

origin
Southwestern USA and Mexico

cultivation
The minimum temperature for the adult plant is 50°F (10°C), although the plant can tolerate somewhat lower temperatures if the soil is dry. It is propagated through seeds.

flowering period
Summer

L

Lobivia marsoneri

tribe
Cacteae

subtribe
Echinocereinae

description
Globular, about 3 inches in diameter, dark grey-green. The plant usually is found in small colonies, with many stems offshooting. There are 18–24 slightly protruding ribs with closely set, grey-white, felt-covered areoles. Each areole has 8–12, yellowish-brown, 1-inch-long, radial spines and as many as 5, slightly longer, central spines, which are hooked at their tips. The flowers are open funnel-shaped, about 2½ inches in diameter and 2 inches long, burnt yellow to reddish. They appear from the sides of the stem.

origin
Argentina

cultivation
The minimum temperature for the adult plant is 50°F (10°C), and it needs partial shade from the direct rays of the sun. The plant is propagated through cuttings or seeds.

flowering period
Summer

Lobivia famatimensis

var. haemathantha

tribe
Cacteae

subtribe
Echinocereinae

description
Globular to very slightly columnar, about 1½–2 inches in diameter, dark green, usually growing in a solitary state. There are 18–24 slightly protruding ribs, covered with closely set, white-felted areoles. Each areole has 8–16, white, ¼-of-an-inch-long, radial spines. The flowers are open funnel-shaped, about 2 inches in diameter and length, and contain many shades of yellow. They grow from the sides of the stem.

origin
Argentina

cultivation
The minimum temperature for the adult plant is 45°F (7°C). It needs full sunlight, and is propagated through seeds.

flowering period
Summer

Lobivia oligotricha
(DRAGON'S BLOOD CACTUS)

◄

tribe
Cacteae

subtribe
Echinocereinae

description
Globular to columnar with a concave apex, dark blue-green, about 6 inches in diameter. There are about 20 ribs spiralling along the stem, further segmented by protruding tubercles where the areoles appear. The white felt-covered areoles have 10–14, ½-an-inch-long, radial spines and as many as 5, longer, heavier, central spines. All the spines are brown to grey. The stem is prone to giving off shoots profusely from its base, forming small colonies. The flowers are bell-shaped, about 1½ inches in diameter and in length, and have bright red petals, cream-coloured stamens, and a short green tube. In general, the flowers remain open for only a few days.

origin
Bolivia

cultivation
The minimum temperature for the adult plant is 50°F (10°C). It needs to be shaded from the direct rays of the sun during the summer, and is propagated through cuttings or seeds.

flowering period
Spring

L

Lophophora williamsii
(WHISKEY BARREL CACTUS)

tribe
Cacteae

subtribe
Echinocactinae

description
Globular with a depressed apex, dark green, about 4 inches tall and somewhat larger in diameter. The plant puts forth many additional stems from its large tap-root. They form tightly spaced colonies. The surface is broken by slightly raised, rounded ribs that are further segmented by irregular horizontal breaks. The areoles are located at the centre of the tubercles and covered with cream-coloured hair tufts. A mass of these tufts fills the centre of the apex. There are no spines. Tubular flowers with pale pink petals grow from the centre of the apex.

origin
Texas and northern Mexico

cultivation
The minimum temperature for the adult plant is 45°F (7°C). Frost is deadly to the plant, which can withstand cold temperatures only if its soil is dry. It is propagated through seeds or shoots.

flowering period
Summer

Lobivia silvestrii
(PEANUT CACTUS)

▲

tribe
Cacteae

subtribe
Echinocereinae

description
A colony-growing plant, often resembling a pile of fuzzy, grey-green peanuts. Stems are 2–6 inches long and as much as 1 inch in diameter. Six to 10 non-protruding ribs have close-set, felt-covered, white to cream areoles. Spines are numerous, but highly variable, resembling bristles. The flowers are about 2 inches long, up to 4 inches in diameter, and appear at the end of scale- and hair-covered tubes. They are bright orange-red with cream to light yellow stamens, and grow from the stem apex. Crossbreeds have resulted in flowers of other colours and dimensions.

origin
Argentina

cultivation
The minimum temperature for the adult plant is 45°F (7°C). The plant needs full sunlight, and significant amounts of water. It is propagated through offsets, as the plant itself is self-sterile. Spider mites are a problem with this species.

flowering period
Spring into mid-summer

Mammillaria baumii
▼

tribe
Cacteae

subtribe
Cactinae

description
From above the plant appears to be encircled by an interwoven arrangement of bristly hair. It grows in colonies, with additional plants branching off from the base. In addition, older plants may sprout branches along the basal level. The oval stem is about 2½ inches in diameter, about 3 inches tall, and dark green in colour. The surface is covered by ½-an-inch tubercles, which are white and felt-covered at their bases. White felt-covered areoles have 28–36 thin radial spines of varying lengths up to ½ an inch. About a half-dozen, slightly longer central spines are white, with shadings of brown. The flowers are funnel-shaped, about 1¼ inches long, and white-tinted with green on the outside and burnt yellow on the inside. The round, greyish fruit is about ½ an inch across.

origin
Mexico

cultivation
The minimum temperature for the adult plant is 50°F (10°C). It needs moderate to full sunlight, and is propagated through seeds or shoots.

flowering period
Summer

Mammillaria camptotricha
▲

tribe
Cacteae

subtribe
Cactinae

description
Globular with a completely rounded apex, dark olive-green, as much as 3 inches in diameter. The surface is broken entirely by ¾-of-an-inch-long, cone-shaped tubercles that point slightly upward. Cream-coloured, felt-covered areoles appear at the tips of the tubercles, each with as many as 8, thin, inch-long, white, radial spines. The spines intertwine with those of the areoles next to theirs. From above, this pattern creates the look of a bird's nest. Cream-coloured, tubular flowers sprout near the bases of the tubercles and rarely extend beyond their tips.

origin
Mexico

cultivation
The minimum temperature for the adult plant is 50°F (10°C), and it needs moderate to full sunlight. The plant is propagated through shoots or seeds.

flowering period
Summer

M

Mammillaria carnea
(PIN-CUSHION CACTUS)

tribe
Cacteae

subtribe
Cactinae

description
Globular with a rounded apex, about 4 inches in diameter, blue-green. The plant tends to put out shoots from its base. Tubercles, which cover the surface of the plant, are 5-sided pyramids with white felt-covered areoles at their tips and a yellowish felt at their bases. There are only 4 central spines to each areole. These are thick, about ¾ of an inch long, grey-white with a black tip, and are slightly curved. The bottommost of the spines is slightly longer. Pale pink flowers grow from the base of the tubercles in a ring around the apex. A brilliant display of red fruit follows.

origin
Mexico

cultivation
The minimum temperature for the adult plant is 50°F (10°C). It is propagated through shoots or seeds.

flowering period
Spring into summer

Mammillaria compressa

tribe
Cacteae

subtribe
Cactinae

description
Globular to columnar with a rounded apex that is slightly concave, blue-green, about 4 inches in diameter and as much as twice that in height. Tubercles are short, squat, and rounded – but not perfectly so. The bases of the tubercles are covered with white felt and short bristles. The areoles are covered with white felt in younger plants but naked in more mature specimens. Each areole has 4–6, red to grey, 1¾–2¾-inch-long, radial spines. Flowers are bell-shaped, about 1½ inches long, with pink to pale purple petals and bright yellow stamens. The fruit is oblong, and red in colour.

origin
Mexico

cultivation
The minimum temperature for the adult plant is 50°F (10°C). It has a wide tolerance for sunlight conditions, and is propagated through shoots.

flowering period
Spring

Mammillaria elongata
(GOLDEN STAR CACTUS)

tribe
Cacteae

subtribe
Cactinae

description
Columnar with a rounded apex, green, ½–1½ inches long and as long as 6 inches. The plant grows in thick colonies, with both erect and prostrate stems. Small tubercles are cone-shaped with yellowish felt areoles, as well as having yellowish felt at their bases. Each areole has as many as 20 short, yellowish, radial spines that intertwine with the spines of their neighbouring areoles, covering the entire surface of the stem. There may be as many as 3, ⅜-of-an-inch-long, central spines, although they are often lacking. The flowers are tubular, about ½ an inch long and yellowish in colour.

origin
Mexico

cultivation
The minimum temperature for the adult plant is 50°F (10°C), and it does not tolerate low temperatures very well. Its soil must be kept dry from mid-autumn through to late winter to avoid rot. The plant is propagated through shoots.

flowering period
Spring into summer

Mammillaria glassii
var. ascensionis

tribe
Cacteae

subtribe
Cactinae

description
Globular, about ¾ of an inch in diameter, dark green. The plant grows in clusters of many versions of itself. Areoles are closely set across the slightly tuberculate surface of the plant, each with 50–70, grey-white, hair-like, ¾-of-an-inch-long, radial spines. These spines intertwine with the spines of the areoles next to their own and with a mass of grey-white, hair-like bristles that grow from the apex, covering the entire surface of the plant. The flowers are open bell-shaped, about ¼ of an inch in diameter, and ¾ of an inch in length, and have off-white to pale pink petals with yellow stamens. They grow near the apex.

origin
Mexico

cultivation
The minimum temperature for the adult plant is 55°F (13°C), and it needs partial shade from the direct rays of the sun and a well-drained soil that has a high mineral content. The plant is propagated through cuttings or seeds.

flowering period
Summer

M

Mammillaria guelzowiana
▼

tribe
Cacteae

subtribe
Cactinae

description
Globular to slightly columnar, about 2½ inches in diameter and as much as 3½ inches tall, dark green. The plant tends to form clusters of offshoots during maturity. The surface of the plant is slightly tuberculate, with a white felt-covered areole appearing on each tubercle. Each areole has from 60–90, ¾-of-an-inch-long, white, hair-like, radial spines and as many as 3, yellowish, ½–¾-of-an-inch-long, central spines that are hooked at their tips. The radial spines intertwine with those of the areoles next to their own, covering the entire surface of the plant. The flowers are open bell-shaped, about 2½ inches in diameter and in length, and have bright pink petals and yellow stamens. They grow from the apex.

origin
Mexico

cultivation
The minimum temperature for the adult plant is 55°F (13°C), and it needs full sunlight, but restricted watering. The plant is propagated through seeds or cuttings.

flowering period
Summer

Mammillaria longimamma
(FINGER MOUND CACTUS)
▲

tribe
Cacteae

subtribe
Cactinae

description
The common name of Finger mound is appropriate for this plant, which resembles a bunch of outward-stretched, short, stubby fingers. The overall shape of the plant is globular when young, becoming more elongated with maturity to a length of about 4 inches. As the plant matures it shoots out additional plants, forming a large cluster. Each stem in this colony-growing plant has a central portion surrounded by outward-radiating, cone-shaped tubercles, each about 1–3 inches long. The base of each of these tubercles is cream, and felt-covered. The areole at the apex of each tubercle is bare and has about 9–12 thin, cream, radial spines, each about ¾ of an inch long. As many as 3 central spines are straight, shorter, and yellow in colour. The flowers are funnel-shaped, about 2½ inches long, and yellow with some reddish tips. The fruit is cone-shaped, pimpled, and orange.

origin
Mexico

cultivation
The minimum temperature for the adult plant is 50°F (10°C), and it needs full sunlight and a large, deep pot to encourage large roots. The plant is propagated through seeds or shoots.

flowering period
Summer

Mammillaria longimamma
var. uberiformis

▼ ▼

tribe
Cacteae

subtribe
Cactinae

description
From above, the mature plant resembles
a layered sunburst. The main stem is
globular, but flattened, and about
2¾ inches tall, with many flattened,
cone-shaped, 1-inch-long tubercles
extending outward. The colour is a blue-
green. Each tubercle carries a cream felt-
covered areole with 4–6, ½-an-inch-
long, yellow, thin, radial spines. The
tubercles resemble daddy-longlegs. The
plant puts out many basal shoots,
becoming clustered. The flowers are
funnel-shaped, about 1½ inches in
diameter, and are red on the outside and
yellow on the inside. They sprout near
the curve of the apex.

origin
Mexico

cultivation
The minimum temperature for the adult
plant is 50°F (10°C), and it needs
moderate to full sunlight and a large pot
to encourage the heavy roots. The plant
is propagated through seeds or shoots.

flowering period
Summer

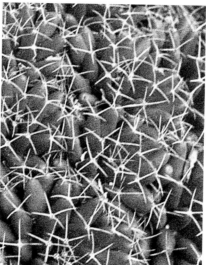

Mammillaria microcarpa
(PINCUSHION CACTUS)

tribe
Cacteae

subtribe
Cactinae

description
Columnar with a rounded apex, dark
green, about 2¼ inches in diameter and
as tall as 6½ inches in the wild (usually
about ⅓ less under cultivation). It has
small, cone-shaped tubercles. The entire
surface of the stem is covered with white
to yellow, ⅜-of-an-inch-long, radial
spines, growing in clusters of as many as
30 from each areole and intertwining
with the spines from all areoles
surrounding it. Each areole also has as
many as 4, ¾-of-an-inch-long, reddish,
central spines, the bottommost of which
is hooked at the tip. The flowers are bell-
shaped with bright pink petals and
orange-yellow stamens, and are about
1½ inches in diameter.

origin
Southwestern USA and northern
Mexico

cultivation
The minimum temperature for the adult
plant is 50°F (10°C). It is propagated
through seeds, but is widely available
as a graft onto other species.

flowering period
Spring into summer

M

Mammillaria prolifera

(LITTLE CANDLES CACTUS)

▼

tribe
Cacteae

subtribe
Cactinae

description
Globular to columnar with a rounded
apex, dark green, about 1½ inches in
diameter and as much as 2½ inches tall.
The plant tends to send out shoots from
its roots, forming very tight colonies that
can extend more than 2 feet in diameter.
The cone-shaped tubercles are about ¼
of an inch in diameter and are arranged
in spirals around the stem. Long, cream-
coloured hairs extend from the base of
the tubercles to above their tips. The
areoles are covered with white to cream-
coloured felt, and they can have dozens
of ¼-of-an-inch-long, thin, white, radial
spines and as many as 10 slightly longer,
yellowish, central spines. The spines of
each areole intertwine with those of the
areoles next to them, largely obscuring
the surface of the stem. Tubular,
yellowish flowers, about ½ an inch long,
grow from the base of the more mature
tubercles. The fruit is oblong, about
½ an inch long, and red.

origin
Cuba and Haiti

cultivation
The minimum temperature for the adult
plant is 55°F (13°C). It is propagated
through shoots.

flowering period
Spring

Mammillaria poselgeri

▲ ▶

tribe
Cacteae

subtribe
Cactinae

description
Globular to columnar stem, curved at the
apex, olive-green, about 1½ inches in
diameter and as much as 6 feet tall.
When the stem reaches its taller extent it
tends to lay, either partially or fully, on
the ground. Stems tend to appear in
groups, each branching from one central
root. The plant is not ribbed but its
surface is covered sporadically with
cone-shaped tubercles, each bearing a
white felt-covered areole, each of which
has 6–10 radial spines, about ½ an inch
long, and yellow to grey-tan. Flowers
appear around the curve of the apex of
mature plants. They are ribbon-like
affairs, about 1½ inches long, bright red,
with significantly extending red style and
stigma and yellow stamen. The fruit is
globular, about ¼–½ an inch in
diameter, and reddish in colour.

origin
California, USA

cultivation
The minimum temperature for the adult
plant is 55°F (13°C), and it needs full
sunlight, interspersed with rest periods.
It is propagated through cuttings.

flowering period
Summer

Mammillaria saboae

◀

tribe
Cacteae

subtribe
Cactinae

description
Globular, about ¾ of an inch in diameter, brilliant dark green. The plant often grows in small clusters of offshoots. The surface of the plant is tuberculate, with a small, triangular, white felt-covered areole appearing at the apex of each tubercle. Widely varying numbers of thin, white, ⅛-of-an-inch-long, radial spines grow from each areole. The flowers are open-petaled, about 1½ inches in diameter and length, with bright pink petals and yellow stemens. They grow near the apex.

origin
Mexico

cultivation
The minimum temperature for the adult plant is 50°F (10°C). It needs full sunlight, and is propagated through cuttings or seeds.

flowering period
Summer

M

Mammillaria setispina
▲

tribe
Cacteae

subtribe
Cactinae

description
The plant grows in colonies of tightly grouped globular or columnar stems, curved at the apex, each with a diameter of about 1½–2¼ inches and a height of 1 foot–1 foot 2 inches. The surface of each stem is notched by cone-shaped tubercles that are white felt-covered at their bases and have off-white areoles at their peak. Each areole has 8–12 white radial spines with darker tips, each about ¾ of an inch long and slightly curved. Central spines, of which there may be as many as 4, are similar but longer – as much as 2 inches each. They have a definite hook at their tips. The flowers emerge along the sides of the mature stems, usually more heavily near the curve of the apex. They are tubular, about 2 inches in length, with irregular petals in various shades of red. The fruit is shaped like a club, about 1 inch long, and is purple to dark red.

origin
Mexico

cultivation
The minimum temperature for the adult plant is 55°F (13°C). It needs full sunlight, but with a rest period throughout the winter at temperatures at around 32°F (0°C). Soil conditions must be well-drained. The plant is propagated through shoots.

flowering period
Summer

Mammillaria sphaerica
▼

tribe
Cacteae

subtribe
Cactinae

description
Globular, curved at the apex, about 1½–2 inches in diameter, blue-green. The surface is covered by ½-an-inch-long, cone-shaped, upward-slanting tubercles set very tightly together. Their bases are encircled by cream felt. The apical areoles have 12–15 cream radial spines that are somewhat darker at the base and about ½ an inch in length. A single central spine is heavier and straight, but only ¼ of an inch long. The areoles of the apex are cream and felt-covered. The flowers are funnel-shaped, about 2½ inches in diameter, and yellow in colour. They generally appear near the curve of the apex. The fruit is oblong, about ¾ of an inch long, and white with a greenish tint and some red flecks.

origin
Mexico

cultivation
The minimum temperature for the adult plant is 50°F (10°C), and it needs full sunlight with a rest period through the winter, during which time it should also have steady mild heat and a limited spraying with water. The plant is propagated through seeds or shoots.

flowering period
Summer

M

Mammillaria theresae
▲

tribe
Cacteae

subtribe
Cactinae

description
Columnar, sometimes branching, with rounded apex, about 1 inch in diameter and 2–3 inches tall, olive-green to purplish. Round tubercles have white felt-covered areoles with 18–24, 1½-inch-long, white, radial spines and 9, slightly longer, central spines. Flowers are tubular, about 1½ inches long, with bright pink petals, bright yellow stamens and a brownish tube.

origin
Mexico

cultivation
The minimum temperature for the adult plant is 55°F (13°C), although the plant can tolerate somewhat lower temperatures over brief periods. It is propagated through seeds.

flowering period
Spring into summer

Mammillaria zephyranthoides
▼

tribe
Cacteae

subtribe
Cactinae

description
Globular with a slightly flattened apex, about 4 inches in diameter and as much as 3½ inches tall. The surface is broken by heavy, cone-shaped tubercles that protrude by as much as an inch. A small, white felt-covered areole grows at the apex of each tubercle, bearing 12–14, thin, white, hair-like, ½-an-inch-long, radial spines and one, yellow, ¾-of-an-inch-long, central spine that is hooked at the tip. Flowers are open-petaled, about 1½ inches in diameter and length, with white or yellow petals and pinkish stamens. They appear around the apex.

origin
Mexico

cultivation
The minimum temperature for the adult plant is 55°F (13°C), and it needs full sunlight. The plant is propagated through seeds.

flowering period
Summer

M

Matucana madisoniorum
▲

tribe
Cacteae

subtribe
Cactinae

description
Globular to slightly columnar, with a rounded slightly concave apex, about 3¼ inches in diameter and as much as 4 inches tall, grey-green to lime-green. There are 7–12 ribs, further divided horizontally by deep furrows, giving an almost tuberculate appearance to the plant. A grey-white felt-covered areole rests at the apex of each tubercle, with "veins" emanating away from it. Only the tubercles around the centre of the apex have spines: 1 red-brown, needle-like, central spine of about 1¼ inches in length, each. The flowers are open-petaled, about 2 inches in diameter, with pink-orange petals with yellow stamens. They appear at the end of a hairy, 4-inch-long tube that grows from the centre of the apex.

origin
Peru

cultivation
The minimum temperature for the adult plant is 62°F (17°C), and it needs partial shading from the direct rays of the sun. The plant is propagated through seeds.

flowering period
Summer

Melocactus matanzanus
▼

tribe
Cacteae

subtribe
Cactinae

description
Globular, about 3½ inches in diameter, pale yellowish-green. There are 8–10 heavily protruding ribs. Along the apical line of each rib, a row of white felt-covered areoles grows, each with 7 or 8 heavy, inward-curving, ¾-of-an-inch-long, radial spines and 1, slightly longer, central spine. All spines are grey-white. The apex has a 3-inch-tall cephalium that is covered with burnt orange to reddish-brown bristles. The flowers are open-petaled, about 2½ inches in diameter and 3½ inches tall, and are bright pink with yellow stamens. They grow from the cephalium.

origin
Cuba

cultivation
The minimum temperature for the adult plant is 61°F (16°C). It needs full sunlight, and is propagated through seeds.

flowering period
Summer

91

Monvillea spegazzinii
▼

tribe
Cacteae

subtribe
Cereinae

description
Columnar with rounded apex, erect or semi-prostrate, about ¾ of an inch in diameter and as long as 6 feet, powdery blue-green. The plant tends to sprout many shoots from its base. There are 3–5 slightly protruding ribs, separated by deep indentations. Small areoles with small amounts of whitish felt grow in alternating lines along the ribs. There are up to 3, ¼-of-an-inch-long, black, radial spines, 2 growing upward and 1 growing downwards and 5 radial spines and 1 longer central spine on more mature parts of the plant. Flowers are bell-shaped, about 5 inches long, with white petals and yellow stamens on the inside surrounded by purplish petals. The petals open widely, but only at night. The flowers grow at the ends of tubes that sprout along the sides of the stem.

origin
Argentina

cultivation
The minimum temperature for the adult plant is 50°F (10°C). It will not tolerate lower temperatures, although it needs partial shade from the direct rays of the summer sun. As it grows – which can be quite a rapid process – the stems need artificial supports. It is propagated through cuttings.

flowering period
Summer

Myrtillocactus geometrizans
◄ ▲

tribe
Cacteae

subtribe
Cereinae

description
Columnar with rounded apex, developing many branches that curve severely upward, yellowish-green, as much as 13 feet tall. However, under cultivation, the plant is much shorter and tends to send out branches from its base. Under these conditions, the branches are about 3–4 inches in diameter. There are 5 or 6 angular ribs separated by deep depressions that display sporadic areas of powdery blue. Areoles are set far apart and have a minimal covering of grey felt. They have 5, ⅛-of-an-inch-long, brown, radial spines and 1, flattened, 1–2¾-inch, black, central spine. The flowers are tubular, about 1¼ inches in diameter, with greenish petals. Several may grow from one areole. The fruit is round, about ¾ of an inch in diameter, pastel blue in colour, sometimes with splotches of green.

origin
Mexico

cultivation
The minimum temperature for the adult plant is 50°F (10°C), and it needs moderate to full sunlight. It is propagated through cuttings.

flowering period
Early summer

N

Neobuxbaumia polylopha
▼

tribe
Cacteae

subtribe
Cereinae

description
Columnar with a rounded, slightly concave apex, about 1–3 feet in diameter and as tall as 42 feet, bright green. There are 15–52 angular ribs, separated by deep depressions. The round areoles are coverd with white felt, and have 6–8, ¾-of-an-inch-long, golden brown, radial spines and 1, 2¾-inch-long, central spine. The spines tend to grow white and fall off as the plant ages. The flowers are tubular, with dark red petals and a scaly tube.

origin
Mexico

cultivation
The minimum temperature for the adult plant is 50°F (10°C). It is propagated through seeds.

flowering period
Early summer

Neodawsonia apicicephalium
▲

tribe
Cacteae

subtribe
Cereinae

description
Columnar with a rounded apex, about 4 inches in diameter and as much as 10 feet tall, pale blue-green. The plant grows in small clusters of basal offshoots. There are 20–30 ribs lined with grey-white felt-covered areoles, each of which has 9–12, inch-long, radial spines and as many as 6, 1½-inch-long, central spines. All spines are grey-white. There is a grey-white to cream-yellow, heavily wool-covered cephalium across the apex. The flowers are open bell-shaped, about 1 inch in diameter and 2 inches in length, and have pinkish petals with yellow stamens. They grow from the cephalium and are nocturnal.

origin
Mexico

cultivation
The minimum temperature for the adult plant is 55°F (13°C). It needs full sunlight, and is propagated through seeds or cuttings.

flowering period
Summer

O

Neowerdermannia vorwerkii

▲

tribe
Cacteae

subtribe
Cereinae

description
Columnar with a rounded apex, as much
as 6 inches in diameter and 24 feet tall,
grey-green. There are as many as 30 ribs,
lined with grey-white felt-covered
areoles. Each areole has 10–14, off-
white, ½-an-inch-long, radial spines and
2–6, yellowish, slightly longer, central
spines. There is a yellowish, woolly
cephalium across the apex. As the plant
matures it grows through the cephalium,
creating a series of bulging areas near
the apex. Flowers are open-petaled,
about 1½ inches long, and pink
with yellow stamens. They grow
from the cephalium.

origin
Mexico

cultivation
The minimum temperature for the adult
plant is 45°F (7°C). The plant needs full
sunlight, and is propagated through
seeds.

flowering period
Summer

Obregonia denegrei
(STARBURST CACTUS)

▼

tribe
Cacteae

subtribe
Echinocactinae

description
Globular, but broken by large,
protruding, teardrop-shaped tubercles
that point outward, bright lime-green,
as much as 5 inches in diameter.
The tubercles have a near-leaf-like
appearance, and can be as much as 1 inch
wide at their base. The small, round,
white felt-covered areoles appear at the
tips of the tubercles. They have 4,
heavily curved, greenish spines, which
fall off as the plant matures. The centre
of the apex is covered with white felt.
White or pinkish flowers, with a scaly
appearance, about 1 inch in diameter,
grow from the apex.

origin
Mexico

cultivation
The minimum temperature for the adult
plant is 50°F (10°C), and it needs full
sunlight and protection from any cold
temperatures or breezes. It is
propagated through seeds.

flowering period
Summer

O

Opuntia erectoclada

tribe
Opuntieae

subtribe
Opuntia

description
Columnar, sometimes prostrate, about 1½ inches in diameter and as much as 2½ inches long, dark green. The plant grows in large clusters of offshoots. The stem is angular with rows of brown felt-covered aeroles along the apex of each angle. Each areole has as many as 4, red-brown, ½-an-inch-long, radial spines. Its flowers are open-petaled, about 1½ inches in diameter, and bright orange-red in colour. They grow from the apex.

origin
Argentina

cultivation
The minimum temperature for the adult plant is 50°F (10°C). It needs partial shading from the direct rays of the sun, and is propagated through cuttings or seeds.

flowering period
Summer

Opuntia erinacea

var. ursina
(GRIZZLY BEAR PRICKLY PEAR CACTUS)

▲

tribe
Opuntieae

subtribe
Opuntia

description
A series of roundish, pad-like joints, each about 3 or 4 inches in diameter and an inch or so thick, growing from a main stem. The entire shrub-like plant grows no more than 2 feet 8 inches tall. It is bright blue-green. Nearly every area of the surface is protected by thin, 2-inch-long, brownish spines that grow in all directions from the large, slightly protruding, white felt-covered areoles. The flowers are bell-shaped, about 2¼ inches long, 2½ inches in diameter, and yellow in colour. The brownish-red and green, oblong fruit is covered with spines.

origin
California, USA

cultivation
The minimum temperature for the adult plant is 45°F (7°C), but it can tolerate lower temperatures if its soil is kept dry. The plant is propagated through cuttings.

flowering period
Mid-summer

Opuntia microdasys

var. albispina
(BUNNY EARS CACTUS)

▼

tribe
Opuntieae

subtribe
Opuntia

description
The plant grows in thick clusters of roundish to teardrop-shaped pads, each 4–6 inches in diameter and ½ an inch or so thick. The overall cluster stands no more than 2 feet tall. The pads are pale olive-green and spotted throughout with areoles covered in cream-coloured glochids, but no spines. Mature plants produce flowers in profusion. These are bell-shaped, about 1½–2 inches long, and yellow in colour. The fruit is round and purplish.

origin
Mexico

cultivation
The minimum temperature for the adult plant is 50°F (10°C), and the plant will not tolerate lower temperatures very well. It is propagated through cuttings.

flowering period
Spring into summer

O

Opuntia tunicata
(CHOLLA CACTUS)

tribe
Opuntieae

subtribe
Cylindropuntia

description
The plant grows as a short bush of erect columnar stems that branch into columnar shoots of as much as 6 inches in length. The overall plant generally grows to about 2 feet in height. All the blue-green stems are covered with alternating rows of white, diamond-shaped areoles with cream-coloured glochids. Six to 12, thick, 1½–2-inch-long, needle-like spines grow from each areole. The spines are red in young plants and cream-coloured in more mature plants, but they are covered with a white sheath that pulls away and clings to nearly anything that comes into contact with it. The flowers are bell-shaped, about 1 inch in diameter, and yellow in colour. The small, reddish fruit is covered with spines.

origin
Mexico

cultivation
The minimum temperature for the adult plant is 50°F (10°C). It is propagated through shoots.

flowering period
Early summer

Oreocereus celsianus
(OLD MAN OF THE MOUNTAINS CACTUS)

tribe
Cacteae

subtribe
Cereineae

description
Columnar with a rounded apex, erect, bright blue-green, about 3–5 inches in diameter and 3 feet tall. The plant tends to send out branches from its base and thus is generally found in small groupings. Each stem has 10–18 rounded ribs, which protrude where the areoles appear. The latter are covered with a little grey-white felt, but also put out tufts of silky, grey-white hairs. Each areole also carries 9, ¾-of-an-inch-long, heavy, cone-shaped, brown, radial spines and as many as 4, heavier, red-brown, central spines that can grow to lengths of 3 inches. The flowers are tubular, with dark pink petals and a hairy tube. They appear near the apex.

origin
Northern South America

cultivation
The minimum temperature for the adult plant is 50°F (10°C). It is propagated through seeds or cuttings.

flowering period
Summer

Pachycereus weberi
▼

tribe
Cacteae

subtribe
Cereinae

description
Columnar with a rounded apex, about
6 inches in diameter and as much as
10 feet tall, pale yellowish-green.
The plant is often found growing in small
groups. There are 12–18 heavily
protruding ribs, lined with brown felt-
covered areoles which are spaced about
¾ of an inch apart. Each areole has
7–9, ½-an-inch-long, radial spines and
as many as 3, 1–2-inch-long, central
spines. All spines are grey to black.
The flowers are tubular, about 3 inches
long, and pink in colour. They grow
from the apex.

origin
Mexico

cultivation
The minimum temperature for the adult
plant is 50°F (10°C). It needs
full sunlight, and is propagated
through seeds.

flowering period
Summer

Oroya peruviana
▲

tribe
Cacteae

subtribe
Echinocactinae

description
Flattened globular, bluish-green, about
6 inches in diameter and 4 inches tall.
There are 12–23 ribs notched into
long tubercles, on which are set the
linear areoles some ½ an inch long.
Comb-like radial spines measure ½ an
inch, and up to 6 central spines measure
1¼ inches. All the spines are yellowish-
brown. The flowers are bell-shaped, about
1 inch long, and are pale pink, yellowish
at the base, and reddish externally.
They grow on or near the apex.

origin
Peru

cultivation
The minimum temperature for the adult
plant is 55°F (13°C), and it needs full
sunlight and a well-drained soil that has a
full concentration of sand and pebbles.
It is propagated through seeds.

flowering period
Mid-summer

P

Parodia brevihamata

▼

tribe
Cacteae

subtribe
Cactinae

description
Globular, about 1½ inches in diameter, dark olive-green. There are 24–32 tuberculate ribs, each with a row of close-set, yellowish felt-covered areoles along the apex of the tubercles. Each areole has 12–16, yellowish, ⅓-of-an-inch-long, radial spines and as many as 6, tan, ¼-of-an-inch-long, central spines. The flowers are open-petaled, about ¾ of an inch in diameter, and bright lemon-yellow in colour.

origin
Brazil

cultivation
The minimum temperature for the adult plant is 50°F (10°C). The plant needs full sunlight, and is propagated through seeds.

flowering period
Summer

Parodia grossei
(PARAGUAY BALL CACTUS)

▼

tribe
Cacteae

subtribe
Echinocactinae

description
Globular to columnar with a rounded and concave apex, bright yellowish-green, 6–10 inches in diameter and as tall as 3 feet 4 inches. There can be as many as 36 thin, sharp ribs. The areoles are close-set, round, and covered with off-white felt near the apex, the centre of which is covered with the same off-white felt. Each areole has 4–10, reddish-brown to grey, curved spines, the longest being about 2 inches. Its flowers are tubular, about 2 inches long and 1½ inches in diameter, with yellow petals that open very widely. They grow from the apex and remain in bloom for about a week.

origin
Argentina and Paraguay

cultivation
The minimum temperature for the adult plant is 55°F (13°C), and it needs only a few hours in the sun each day, followed by partial shading for the rest of the time. It is propagated through seeds.

flowering time
Spring into summer

Parodia haselbergii
(SCARLET BALL CACTUS)

▼

tribe
Cacteae

subtribe
Echinocactinae

description
Globular to slightly columnar with a rounded but slightly concave apex, often semi-prostrate when columnar, dark green, 2–4 inches in diameter and as long as 5 inches. There are more than 30 ribs, sporting roundish tubercles. Each tubercle bears small, white felt-covered areoles, each with about 2 dozen thin, yellow to white, ⅜-of-an-inch-long, radial spines and 3–5, longer, yellow, central spines. The radial spines intertwine with those of the areoles adjacent to them, covering the entire surface of the stem. Its flowers are water-lily-like, bright reddish-orange, growing on short tubes near the stem's apex.

origin
Brazil

cultivation
The minimum temperature for the adult plant is 50°F (10°C), and the plant does best if partially shaded from the direct rays of the sun. It is propagated through seeds.

flowering period
Spring into summer

P

Pelecyphora aselliformis

▼

tribe
Cacteae

subtribe
Cactinae

description
Globular to columnar, about 2 ¼ inches in diameter and as much as 4 inches tall. The surface of the stem is grey-green, but it is largely covered by a pattern of areoles that resemble white, fossilized ferns or modernday ferns covered with frost. They are located on tubercles that protrude by about ¼ of an inch and are arranged spirally around the stem. The areoles put out additional cream-coloured wool that covers much of the space between them and they also sport a large number of tiny, short spines. The flowers are bell-shaped, about 1 inch in diameter, with white outer petals and reddish-purple inner petals. They grow at the apex. The stem tends to put out shoots from around the apex.

origin
Mexico

cultivation
The minimum temperature for the adult plant is 55°F (13°C), and it needs full sunlight, but with a well-defined rest period during the winter. It also needs regular, but limited watering. The plant is propagated through seeds or cuttings, but is very slow growing.

flowering period
Summer

Pereskia lychnidiflora

▲

tribe
Pereskia

subtribe
Pereskia

description
A completely tree-like species, as much as 36 feet tall. The many branches form a heavy canopy of green and the leaves are 1½-3 inches long. The areoles along the stem and branches are covered with black felt and have 1 central spine that can be as long as 2 inches. The flowers are open-petaled, about 2½ inches in diameter, and are bright orange with yellow stamens. They appear at the ends of the branches.

origin
Mexico

cultivation
The minimum temperature for the adult plant is 55°F (13°C), and it needs full sunlight. It is propagated through cuttings or seeds.

flowering period
Summer

R

Pilosocereus purpusii
(WOOLLY TORCH CACTUS)

◀

tribe
Cacteae

subtribe
Cereinae

description
Columnar with many branches, sometimes prostrate, about 1½ inches in diameter and as long as 10 feet. There are 12 ribs, each with a row of close-set, white felt-covered areoles that also sport long, wispy hairs. The spines vary widely in number, but are generally yellowish in colour and as long as 1 inch. There is also a white, woolly cephalium on top of the apex, from which the flowers grow. These are open funnel-shaped, about 1 inch in diameter, 3 inches in length, and are pale pink. They are also nocturnal.

origin
Mexico

cultivation
The minimum temperature for the adult plant is 50°F (10°C), and it needs full sunlight. The plant is propagated through cuttings or seeds.

flowering period
Summer

Polaskia chichipe

▼

tribe
Cacteae

subtribe
Cereinae

description
Columnar, heavily branching from basal offshoots, about 3 inches in diameter and as much as 16 feet tall. There are 6–12, heavily protruding ribs, with swellings where the grey felt-covered areoles appear. The areoles are about ¾ of an inch apart on the rib and have 6–8, ½-an-inch-long, radial spines and 1, ¾-of-an-inch-long, central spine. All spines are dark grey to black. The flowers are widely open-petaled, with protruding stamens, about 1½ inches in diameter and in length, and are yellowish-white to greenish-white. They grow from the sides of the apex.

origin
Mexico

cultivation
The minimum temperature for the adult plant is 55°F (13°C). It needs full sunlight, and is propagated through seeds or cuttings.

flowering period
Summer

Rebutia fabrisii

▲

tribe
Cacteae

subtribe
Echinocereinae

description
Globular, about ¾ of an inch in diameter, pale olive-green. The plant grows in heavy clumps of offshoots, and there are as many as 14 tuberculate ribs, spiralling around the sides of the stem. Each rib is lined by closely set, white felt-covered areoles, each with many, ⅛-of-an-inch-long, yellowish-white radial spines that intertwine with the spines of the neighbouring areoles, covering the surface of the plant. The flowers are open-petaled, about 1½ inches in diameter, 1 inch in length, and with bright red petals and bright yellow stamens. They grow from the slightly concave apex.

origin
Argentina

cultivation
The minimum temperature for the adult plant is 45°F (7°C), and it needs full sunlight. The plant is propagated through cuttings or seeds.

flowering period
Summer

Rebutia minuscula

tribe
Cacteae

subtribe
Echinocereinae

description
Globular, but with a depressed apex, dark green, about 2 inches in diameter and ¾ of an inch tall. The plant tends to send out many shoots from its base, resulting in a colonial mound of many related plants. Slightly protruding, angular tubercles are arranged in 16–24 spirals around the stem. The areoles are covered with white felt and thin hairs. They produce 2 or 3 dozen thin, white, quill-like spines, each about ¼ of an inch long. The radial and central spines are exactly alike. Its flowers are bell-shaped, about 1½ inches long, and bright reddish-orange. They grow from the base in great profusion and remain intact for several days.

origin
Argentina

cultivation
The minimum temperature for the adult plant is 45°F (7°C), and the plant cannot tolerate lower temperatures. It requires a strict rest period during the winter, with protection from low temperatures. The plant is propagated through cuttings or seeds.

flowering period
Summer

Rhipsalidopsis rosea

tribe
Cacteae

subtribe
Rhipsalidinae

description
The erect stems are circular to angular, with 4 or 5 sides, and pale green or brownish-green. These end in flat, oakleaf-like sections that are about 1½ inches long. Small, hairy areoles grow along the scalloped edges of these terminal sections. One larger areole appears at the tip of each section, providing for new growth and the floral bloom. As many as 3 pond-lily-like flowers may grow from each areole, but once only. These are about 1½ inches in diameter, and bright powdery pink.

origin
Brazil

cultivation
The minimum temperature for the adult plant is 45°F (7°C). It needs to be partially shaded from the direct rays of the sun and also needs a rest period during the winter, when waterings are reduced but mist sprayings are continued. It is propagated through cuttings.

flowering period
Spring and early summer

S

Schlumbergera opuntioides
▼

tribe
Cacteae

subtribe
Epiphyllinae

description
Branching, heavily segmented into flattened sections that are about ¾ of an inch wide and 2 inches long, dark green. The surface of each segment is covered with rows of white felt-covered areoles, each of which has a widely varying number of tiny, off-white, radial spines. The flowers are tubular with backward-curling petals, about 1¾ inches long, and red with areas of white.

origin
Brazil

cultivation
The minimum temperature for the adult plant is 55°F (13°C). It needs partial shading from the direct rays of the sun and will bloom best if given a short non-watered period just before flowering. It is propagated through cuttings or seeds.

flowering period
Late spring

Strombocactus disciformis
▲

tribe
Cacteae

subtribe
Echinocactinae

description
Globular with a slightly flattened apex, from 2–5 inches in diameter, grey-brown. There are 12–18 tuberculate ribs that spiral around the surface of the plant with olive-green depressions between them, giving the surface a distinctly turtle-shell appearance. Each tubercle has a white felt-covered areole at its apex, with as many as 5 greyish-white, ¾-of-an-inch-long, radial spines. Flowers are open funnel-shaped, about 1½ inches in diameter and slightly less in length. They are creamy yellow in colour.

origin
Mexico

cultivation
The minimum temperature for the adult plant is 50°F (10°C), and it needs full sunlight and carefully restricted watering, and no water during the winter. It is propagated through seeds.

flowering period
Summer

T

Sulcorebutia rauschii

▼

tribe
Cacteae

subtribe
Echinocereinae

description
Globular with a slightly concave apex, about 1 inch in diameter, silvery green. The plant grows in small clusters of basal offshoots. There are as many as 16 ribs divided into 6-sided tubercles. At the darker centre of each tubercle there is a naked areole with about 12, thin, ¹⁄₁₆-of-an-inch-long, yellowish, radial spines and as many as 2, slightly longer, central spines. The flowers are open-petaled, about 1 inch in diameter and the same in length, with bright pink petals and creamy yellow stamens.

origin
Bolivia

cultivation
The minimum temperature for the adult plant is 50°F (10°C). The plant needs full sunlight, and is propagated through cuttings or seeds.

flowering period
Mid-summer

Thelocactus conothele

var. macdowellii

▼

tribe
Cacteae

subtribe
Cactinae

description
Globular, about 4 inches in diameter, bright green. There are 8–10 heavily protruding ribs, further divided horizontally into tubercles. Each tubercle has a white felt-covered areole with 8–18, thin, grey-white, 1-inch-long, radial spines and as many as 4, reddish, 2-inch-long, central spines. The flowers are open bell-shaped, about 2–2½ inches in diameter and length, with bright pink petals and yellow stamens. They grow from the apex.

origin
Mexico

cultivation
The minimum temperature for the adult plant is 50°F (10°C). The plant needs full sunlight, and is propagated through seeds.

flowering period
Summer

Thelocactus lophothele

tribe
Cacteae

subtribe
Cactinae

description
Globular to columnar, about 2 inches in diameter and as much as 10 inches tall. The plant tends to grow in clusters of basal offshoots. There are 16–20 ribs spiralling along the sides of the plant and further divided horizontally into irregular, lava-like tubercles. A grey-tan felt-covered areole sits on top of the apex of each tubercle with 3–6, heavy, reddish-brown, 1-inch-long, radial spines. The flowers are open funnel-shaped, about 2 inches in diameter, and bright lemon-yellow. They grow from the grey-tan felt-covered centre of the apex.

origin
Texas and Mexico

cultivation
The minimum temperature for the adult plant is 42°F (6°C). It needs partial shade from direct sunlight, a compost-enriched soil and limited watering. The plant is propagated through cuttings or seeds.

flowering period
Summer

Thelocactus rinconensis
var. phymatothele

tribe
Cacteae

subtribe
Cactinae

description
Globular to columnar with a flattened or concave apex, from 3–6 inches in diameter, greyish-green. There are 13 heavily protruding ribs, further divided horizontally into angular tubercles. The areole at the apex of each tubercle has from 0–3, ¼-of-an-inch-long, grey, radial spines. The flowers are open funnel-shaped, about 1½ inches long, and pinkish-white.

origin
Mexico

cultivation
The minimum temperature for the adult plant is 50°F (10°C), and it needs full sunlight and a limestone-rich soil. It is propagated through seeds.

flowering period
Summer

U

Trichocereus thelogonus

tribe
Cacteae

subtribe
Cereinae

description
Columnar, generally prostrate or only semi-erect, about 2–3 inches in diameter and as long as 5 feet, pale olive-green. There are about 12, heavily protruding, tuberculate ribs. Each tubercle has a tan felt-covered areole with as many as 6, ½-an-inch-long, radial spines and 1, 1½-inch-long, central spine. All the spines are yellowish to greyish. The flowers are funnel-shaped to open-petaled, about 8 inches in diameter (when open) and about the same in length. They are white in colour and are nocturnal.

origin
Argentina

cultivation
The minimum temperature for the adult plant is 50°F (10°C), and it needs full sunlight. The plant is propagated through cuttings or seeds.

flowering period
Summer

Uebelmannia pectinifera

tribe
Cacteae

subtribe
Echinocactinae

description
Globular to slightly columnar, about 5 or 6 inches in diameter and as tall as 1½ feet, greyish-brown. There are 16–20 heavily protruding ribs, and the apex of each is lined with a row of closely set, brown felt-covered areoles, with varying numbers of ¾-of-an-inch-long, brown, central spines. These spines protrude directly outward, giving the apex of each rib the appearance of a Mohawk haircut. Flowers are open-petaled, about ½ an inch in diameter, and lemon-yellow in colour. They grow from the apex.

origin
Brazil

cultivation
The minimum temperature for the adult plant is 59°F (15°C). It needs full sunlight and a well-drained soil that has a high content of limestone. The plant is propagated through seeds.

flowering period
Summer

Wilcoxia poselgeri
▶

tribe
Cacteae

subtribe
Cereinae

description
Bush-like, heavily branching, about
¾-of-an-inch in diameter and as long as
2 feet, olive-green. There are 8–10 ribs
with closely set, off-white felt-covered
areoles. Each areole has 8–12, ⅛-of-an-
inch-long, grey-white, radial spines and
as many as 2, ¼-of-an-inch-long, central
spines. Its flowers are open-petaled,
about 2 inches in diameter and length,
and are purplish-pink. They grow from
the sides of the stem.

origin
Texas and Mexico

cultivation
The minimum temperature for the adult
plant is 50°F (10°C), and it needs partial
shading from the direct rays of the
sun. It is propagated through
cuttings or seeds.

flowering period
Summer

Glossary

apex
Upper side of the tubercle from which the flowers or wool rise; also, more generally, top of the plant.

areole
Cushion-like growing point of the cactus.

bristle
Stiff hair or soft, flexible spine.

callus
Hardened plant tissue which forms over a cut or wound.

calyx
The outer ring of the flower, a floral tube or cup.

cephalium
Densely, woolly, bristly "head" on certain cacti.

epidermis
Outer cell layer of the plant.

epiphyte
Plant growing on another, but not parasitic.

glochid
Barbed hair or bristle.

hybrid
Plant created through the cross-fertilization of two species.

nocturnal
Flowers that open at night only.

offset
Side shoot capable of producing a new plant.

perennial
A plant that continues to grow from year to year.

pistil
Female part of the flower consisting of the ovary, style, and stigma.

radial spines
Spines set around the edge of the areole.

ribs
Sections of the stem forming raised ridges, usually vertical.

serrate
Saw-edged.

stamen
Male part of the flower consisting of the filament or stalk and the anther which contains the pollen.

stigma
The terminal part of the ovary, at the end of the style, where pollen is deposited.

style
Stalk-like portion of the pistil. It connects the stigma with the ovary.

succulent
Any plant which stores water in the leaf, root or stem.

tubercle
Small wart-like swelling or growth.

vascular
Having vessels that conduct and circulate liquids.

Index

PICTURE CREDITS

T: top B: bottom L: left R: right M: middle

All pictures were supplied by Dr Charles
Glass, apart from the following:

Premaphotos Wildlife (K.G. Preston-
Mafham): p107L.
Ro-Ma Stock (Robert Marlen): p8T, 9BL, 13,
14, 16B, 17, 18, 20, 25.
Visuals Unlimited (John D. Cunningham):
p11ML, 11BL.
Visuals Unlimited (John Gerlach): p6.
Visuals Unlimited (J. Mauseth): p8B, 19B,
22T, 27, 28.
Visuals Unlimited (Glenn M. Oliver): p9ML.
Visuals Unlimited (Doug Sokell): p15.
Visuals Unlimited (John N. Trager): p9T, 9BR,
10T, 10B, 11R, 12, 16T, 19T, 22B, 24.